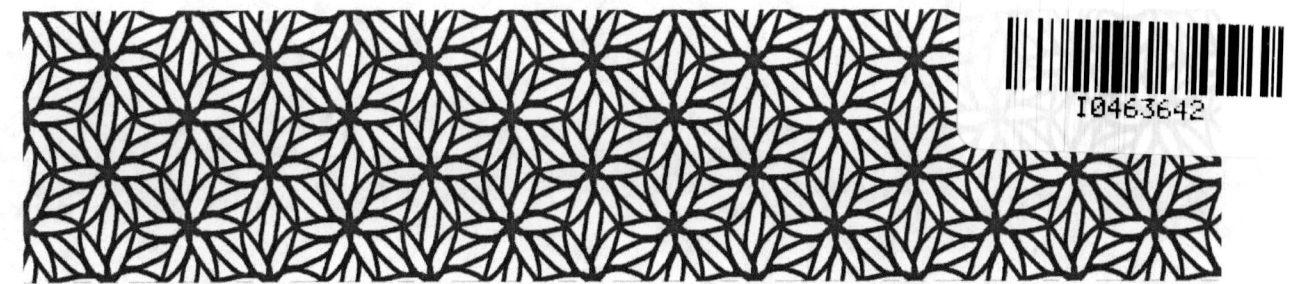

Delicate Pattern
adult coloring book
Volume 1

by Kreativ Corner

Delicate Pattern Coloring Book, Volume 1
©2017 Kreativ Corner

www.kreativcorner.net

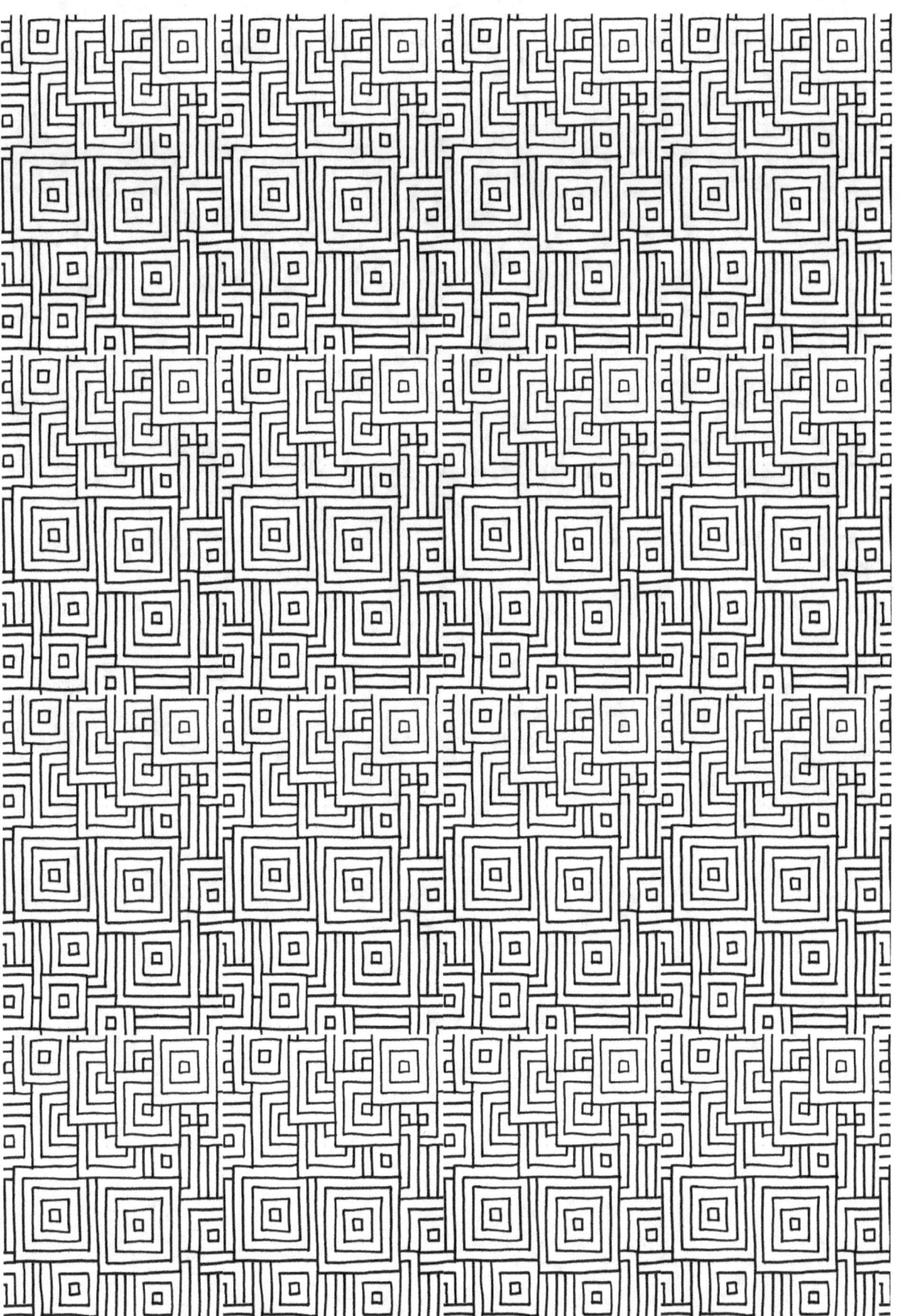

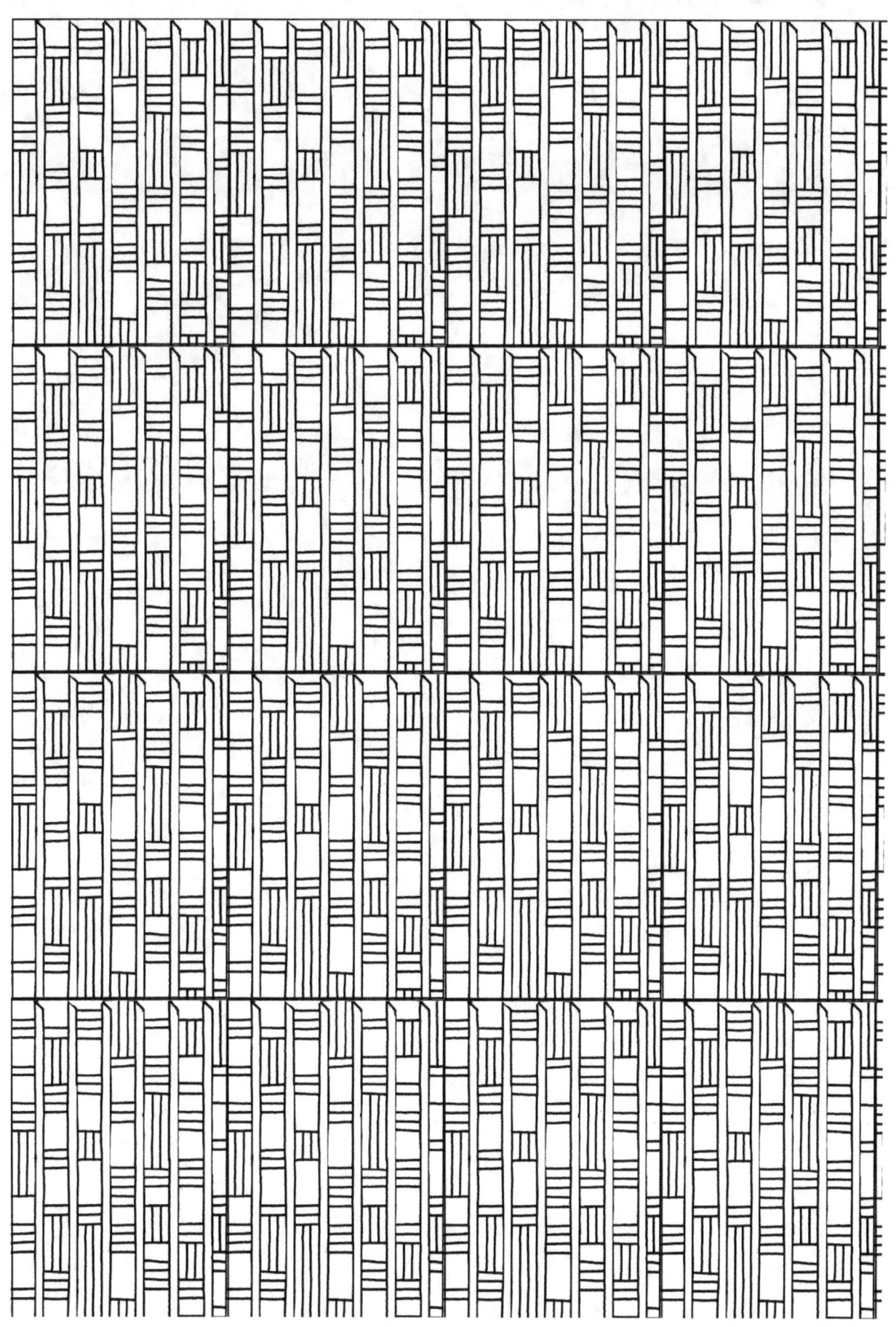

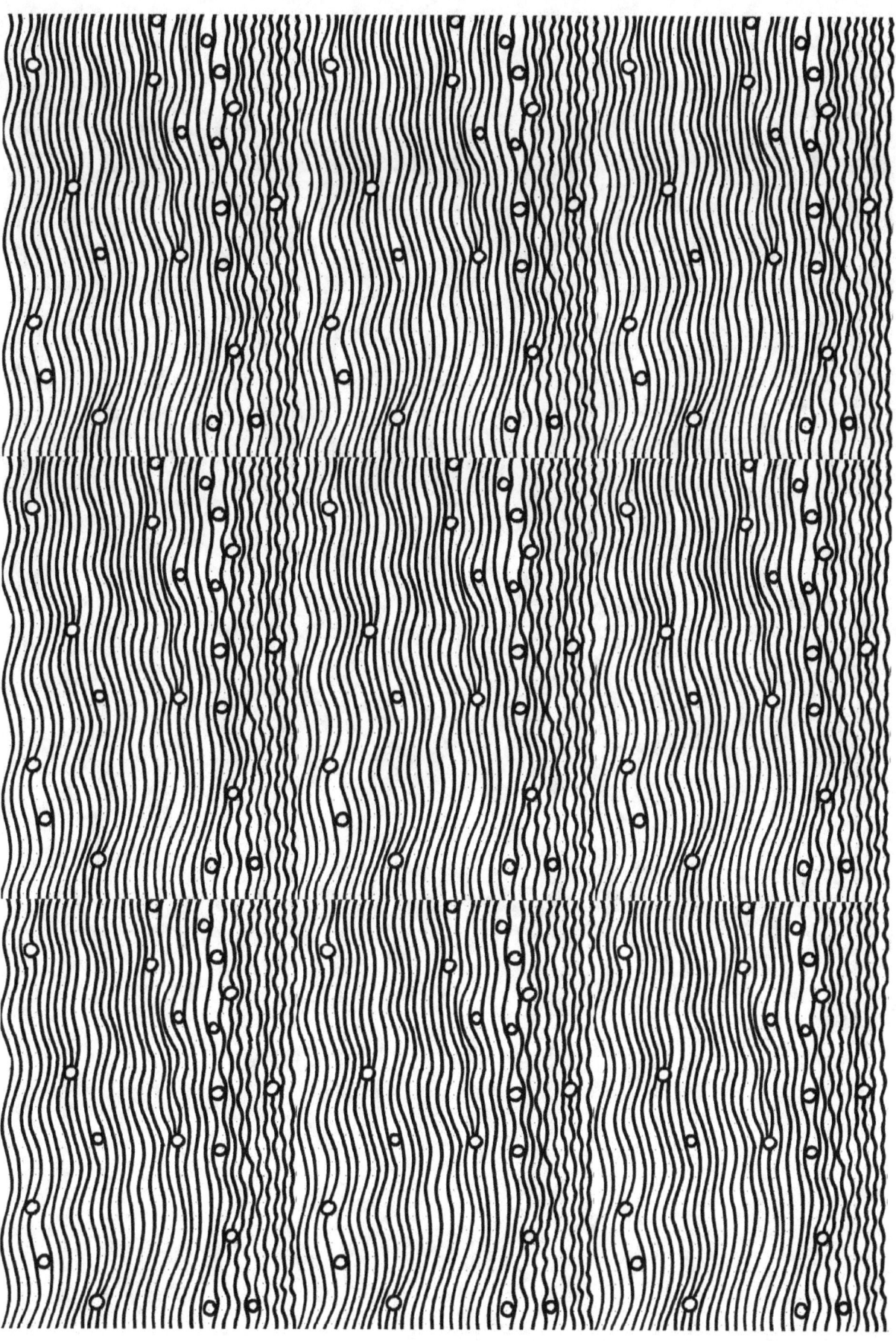

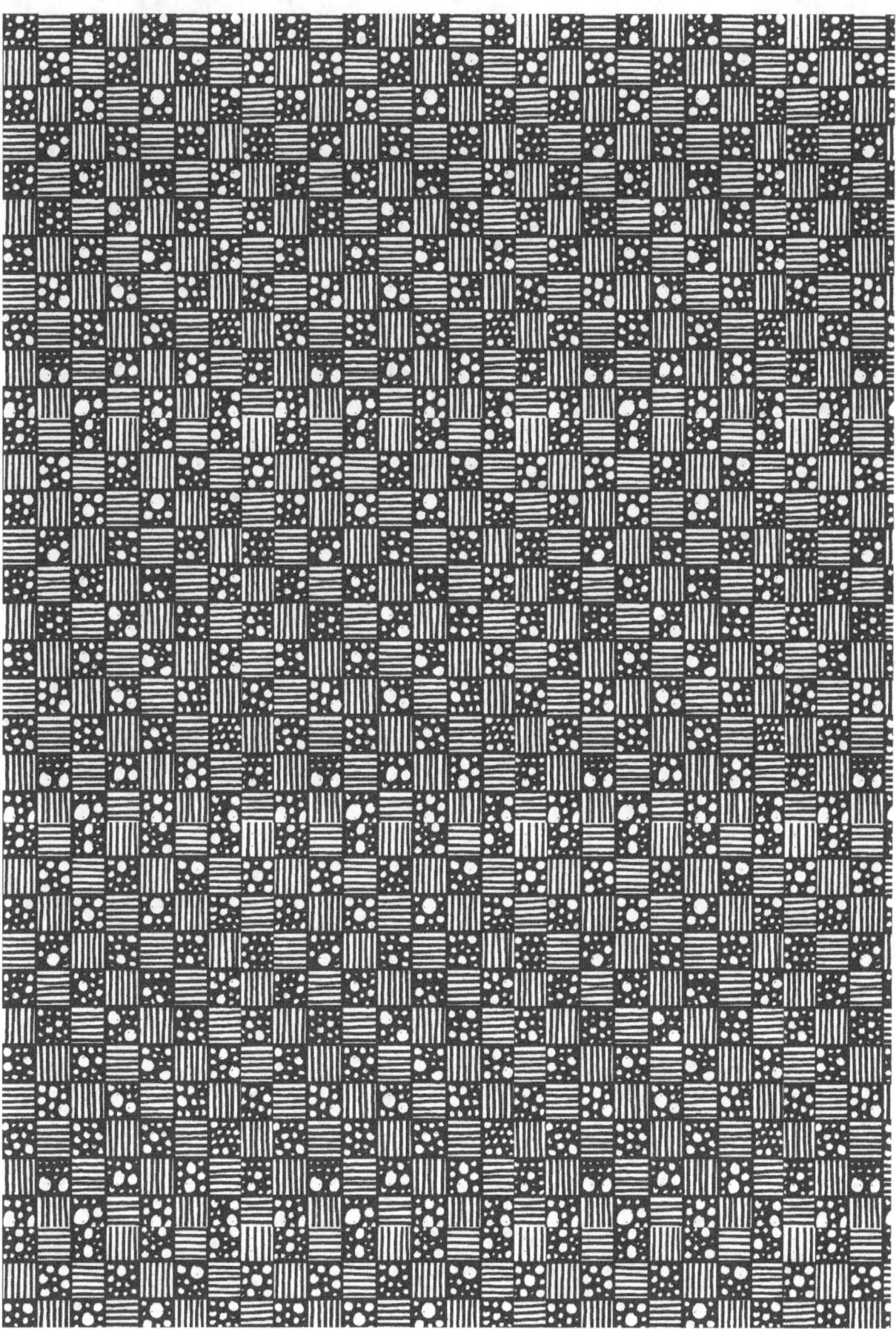

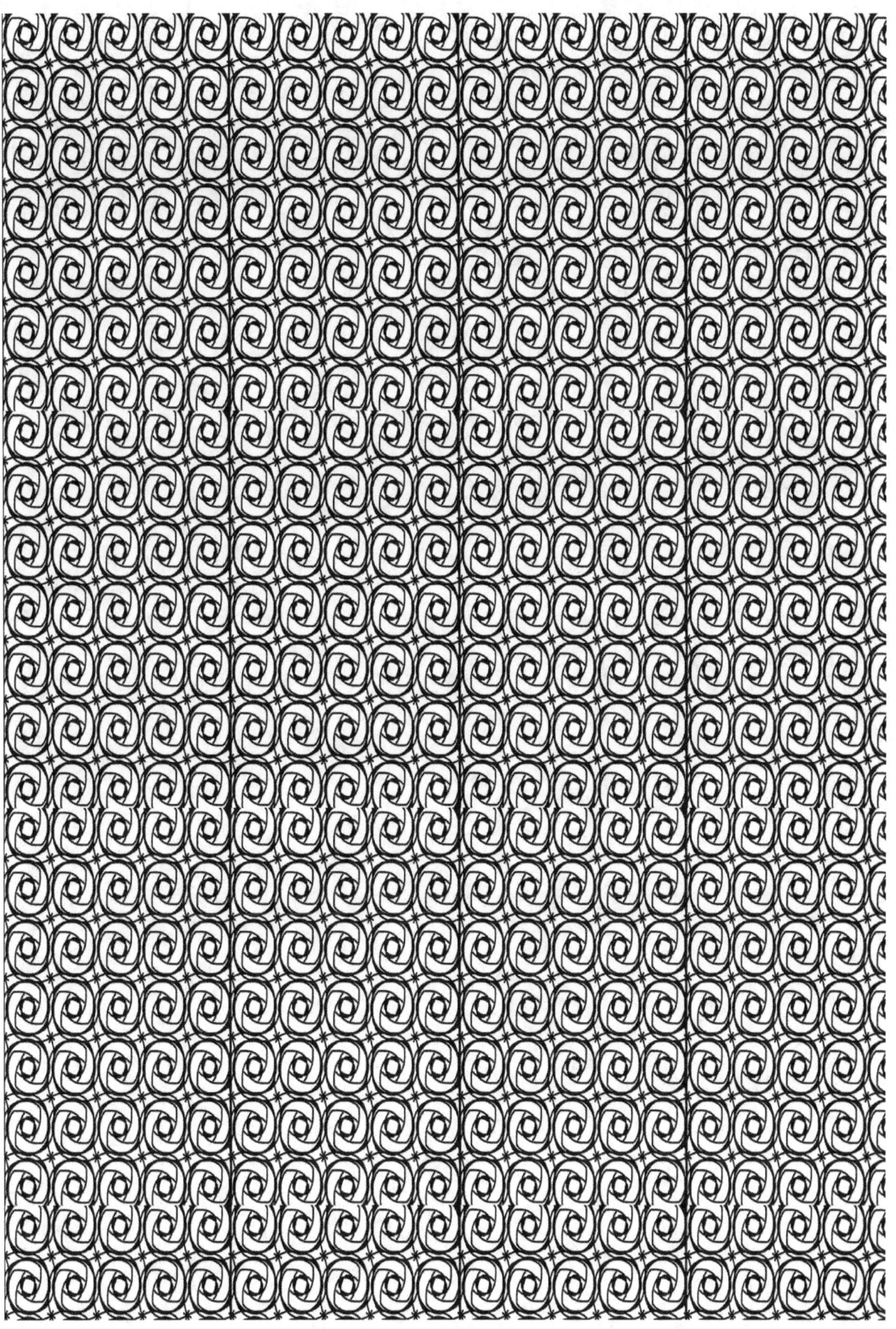

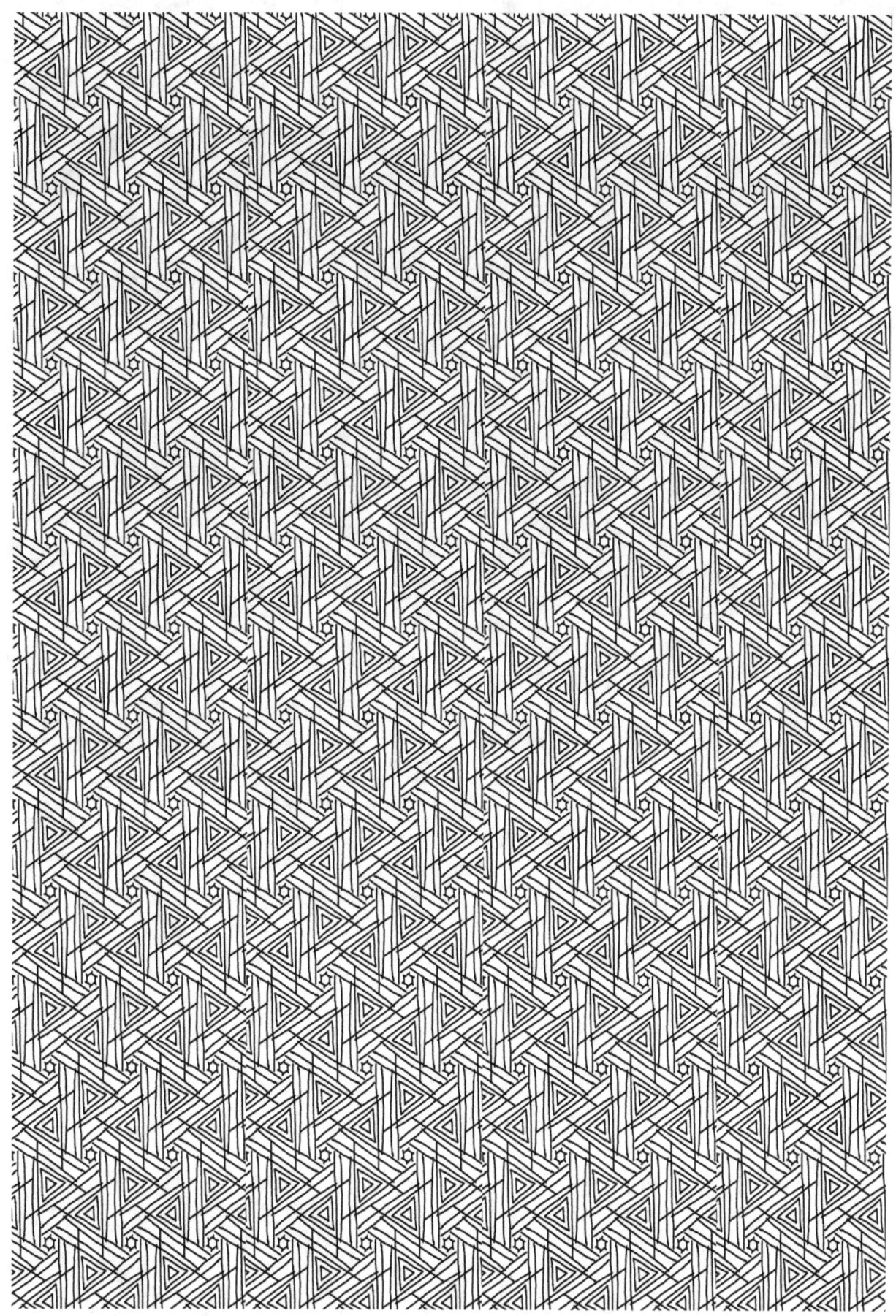

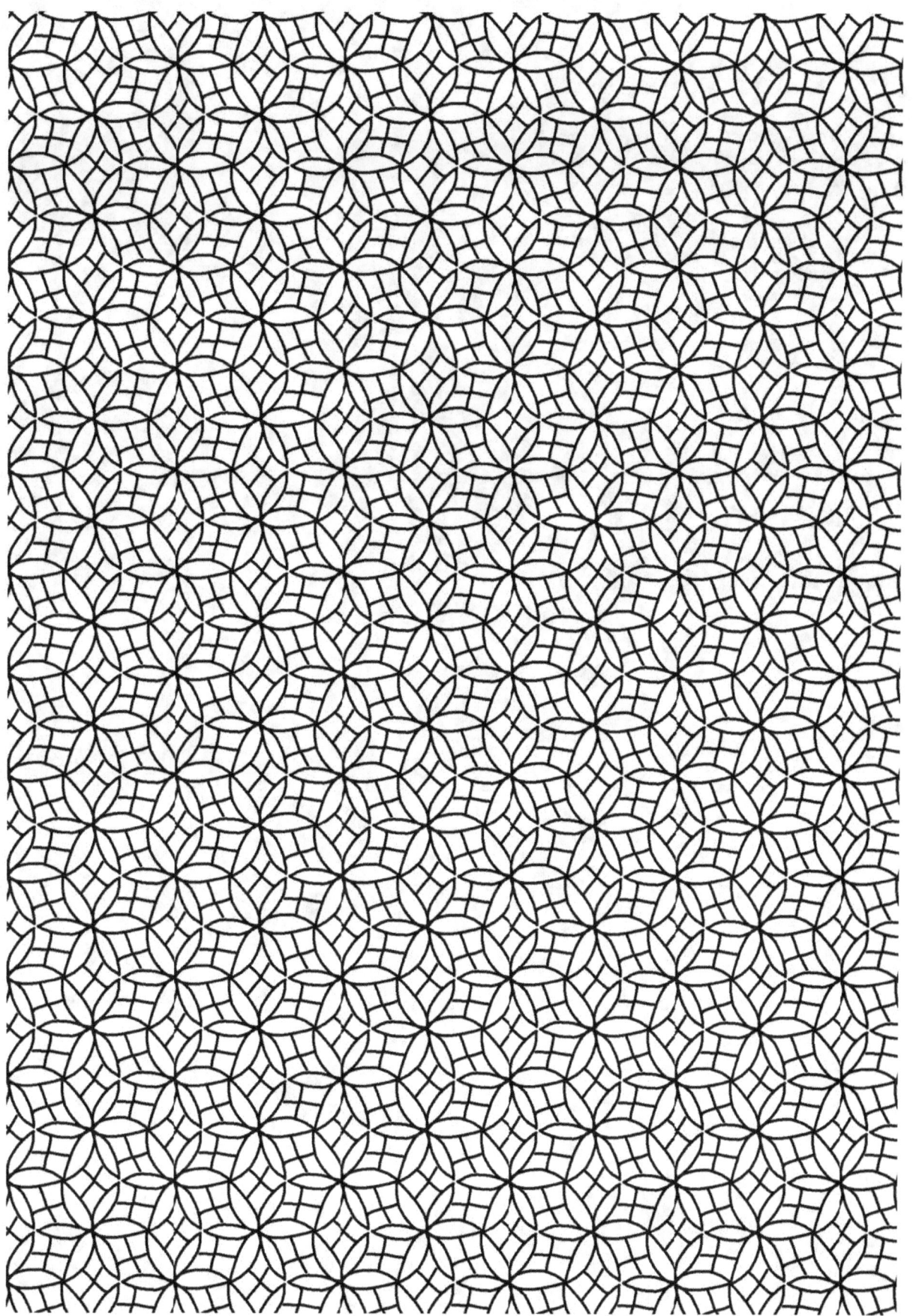

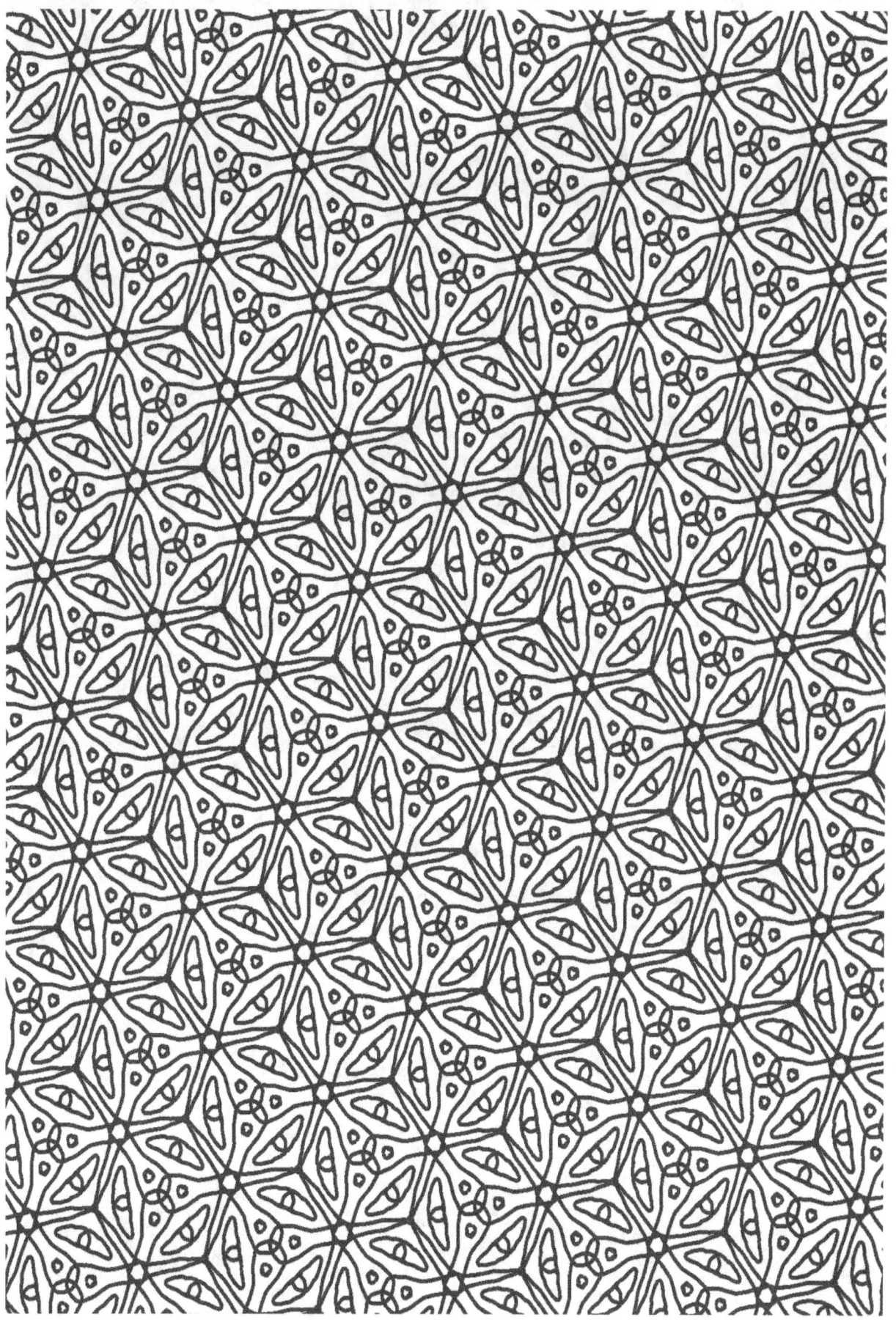

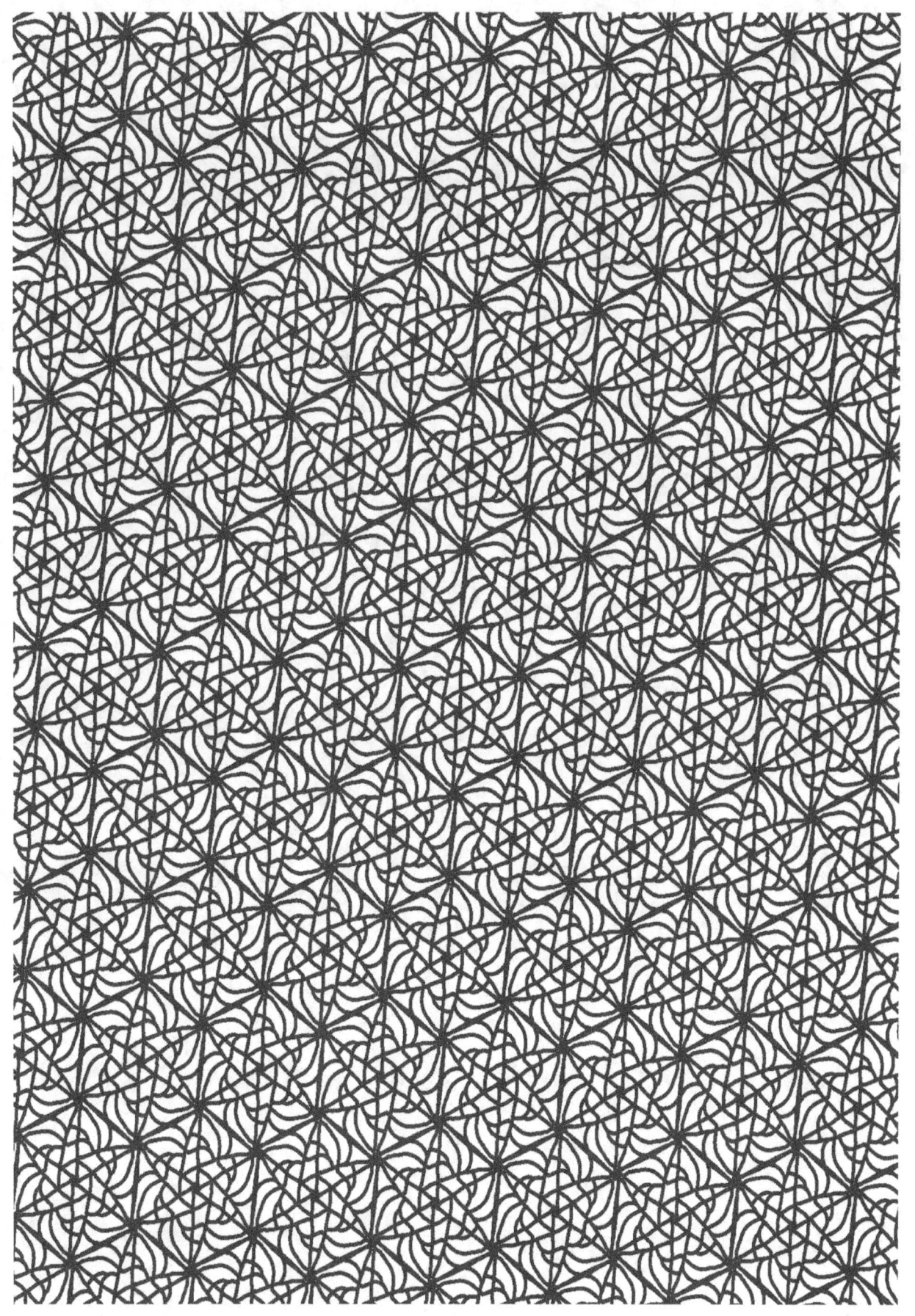

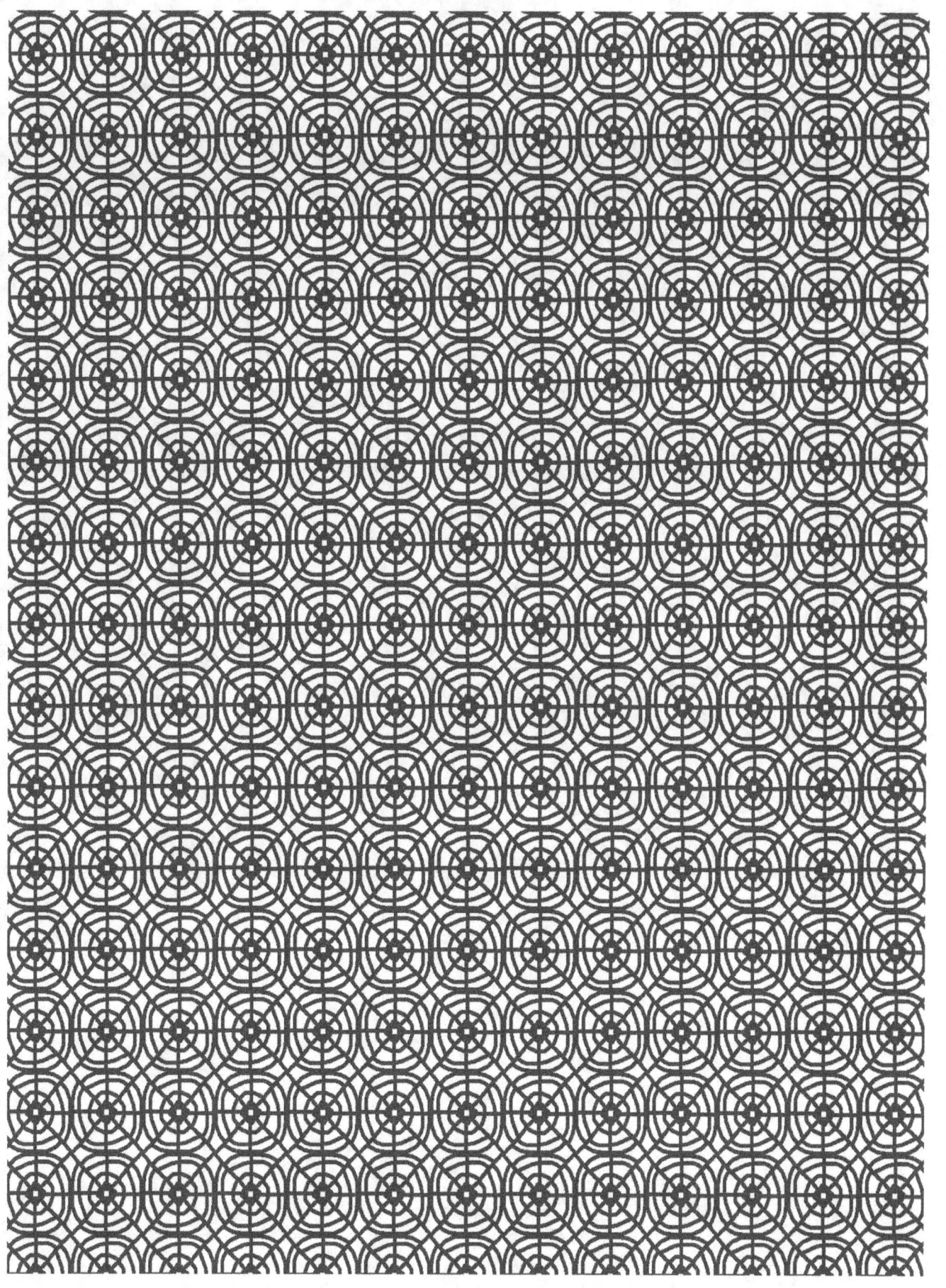

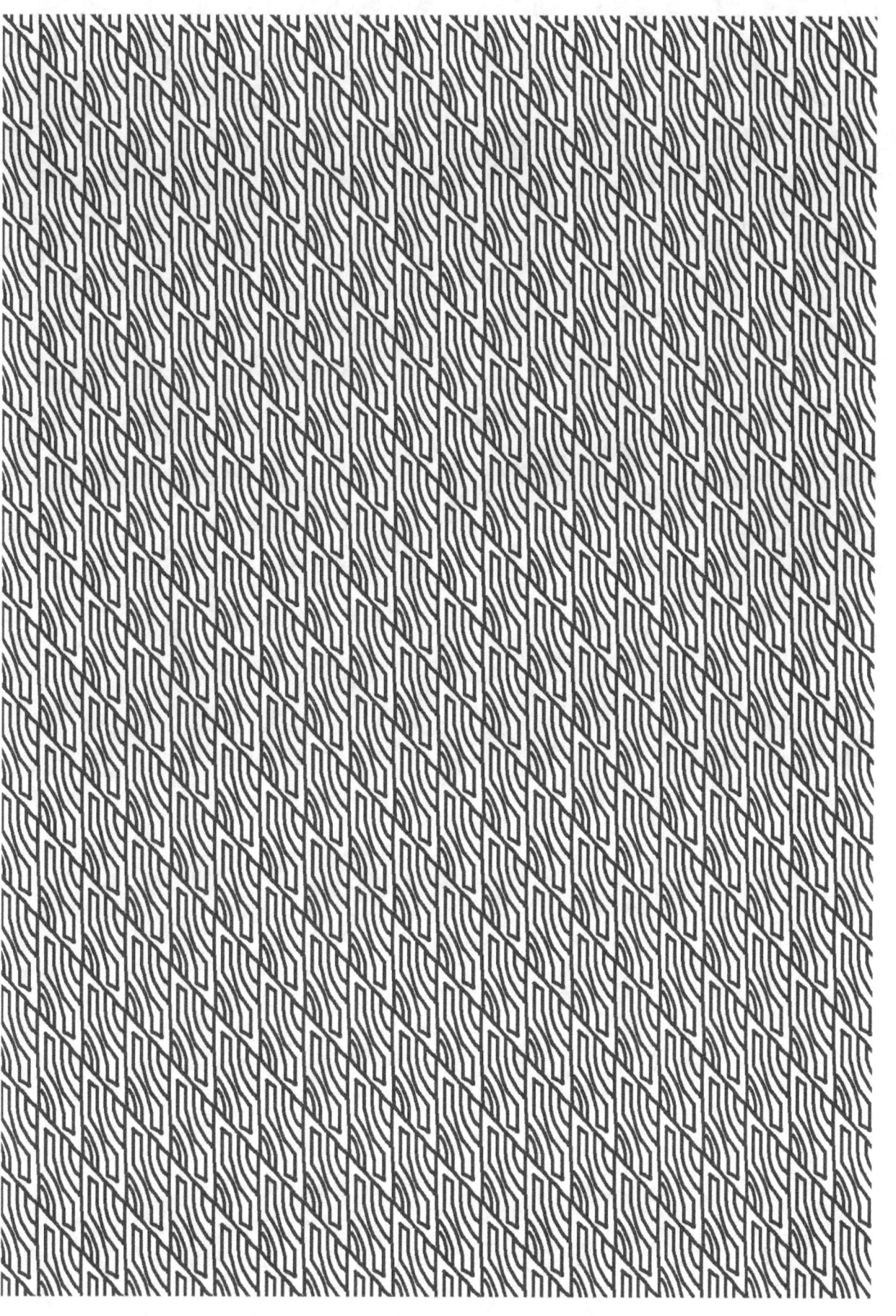

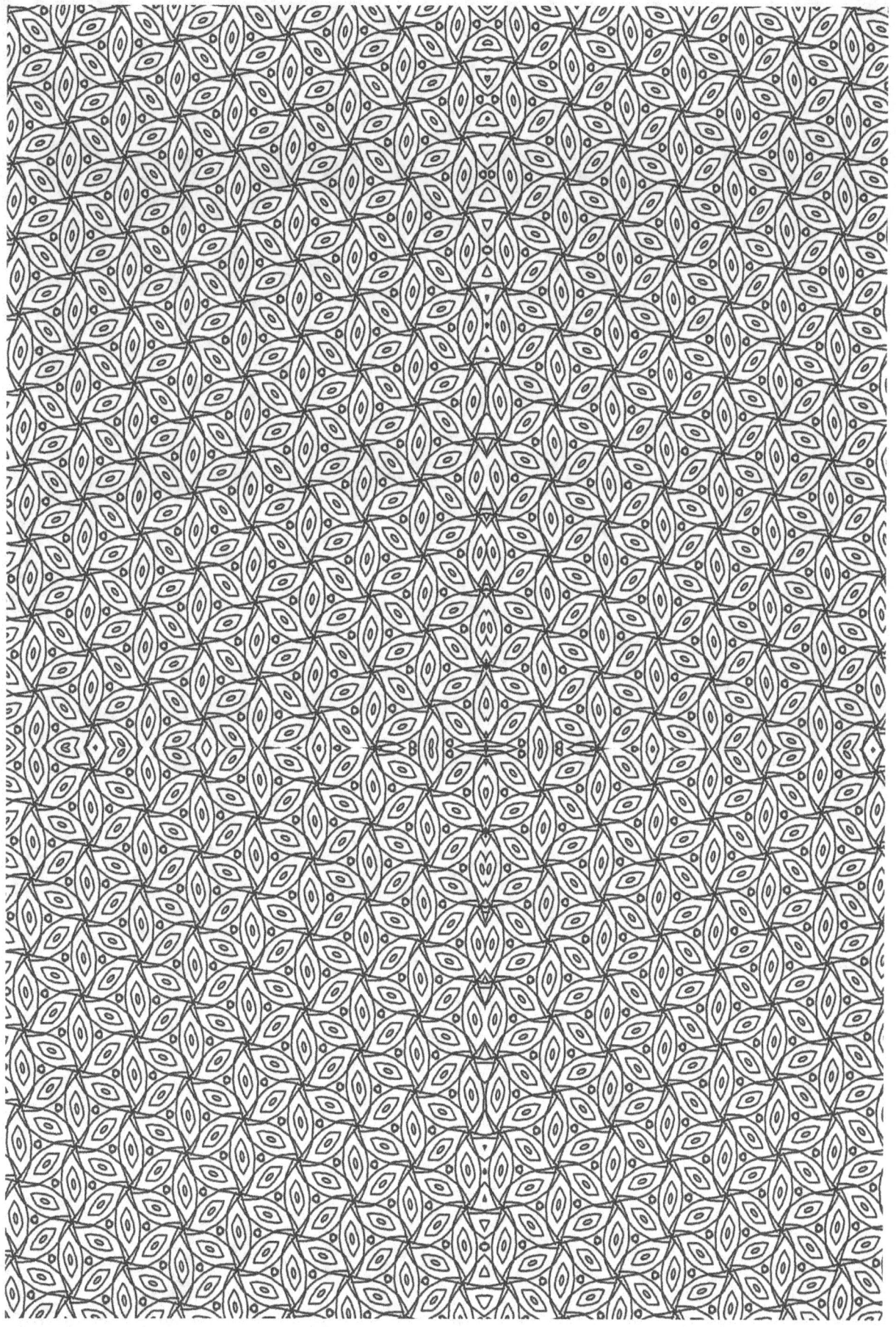

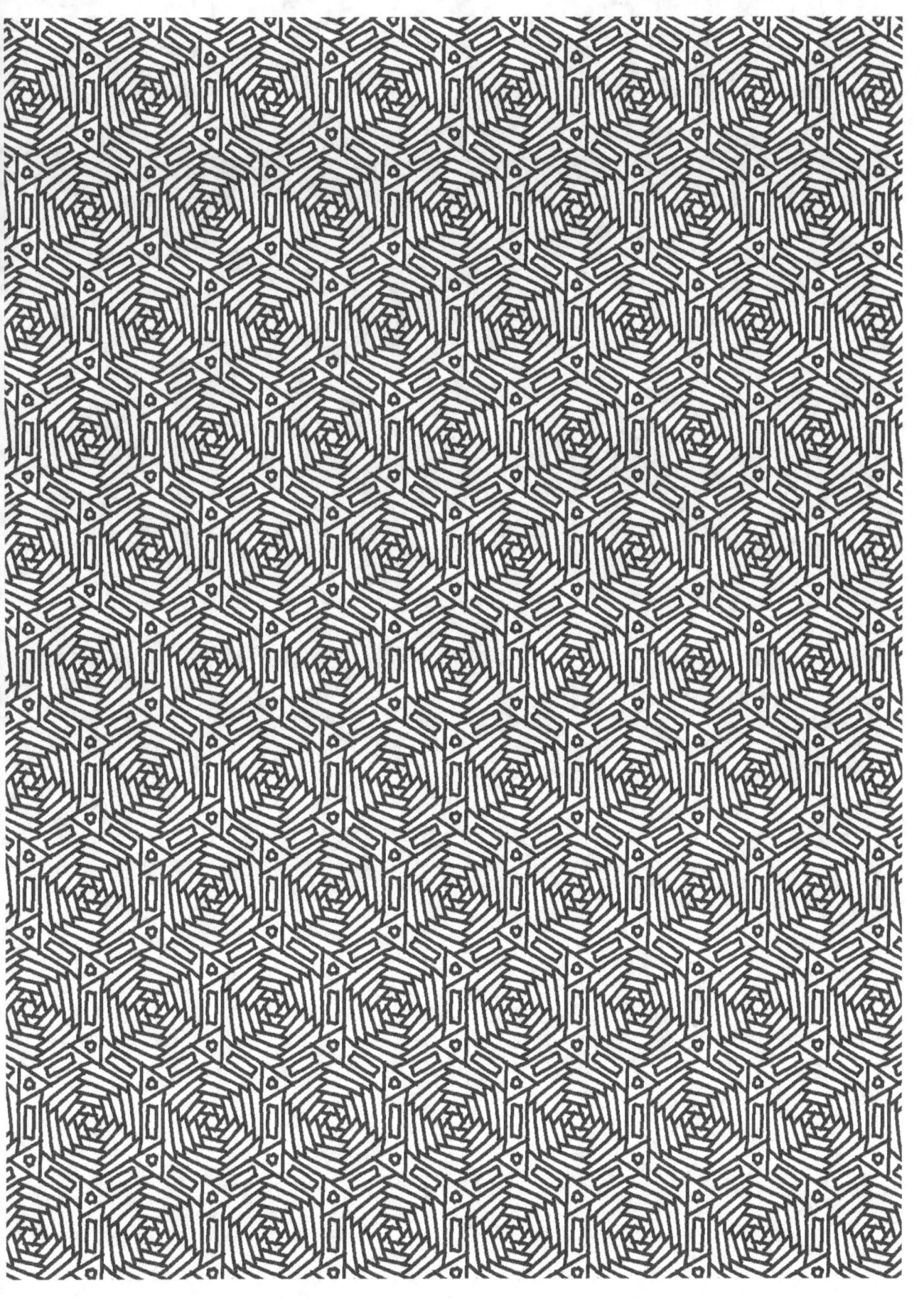

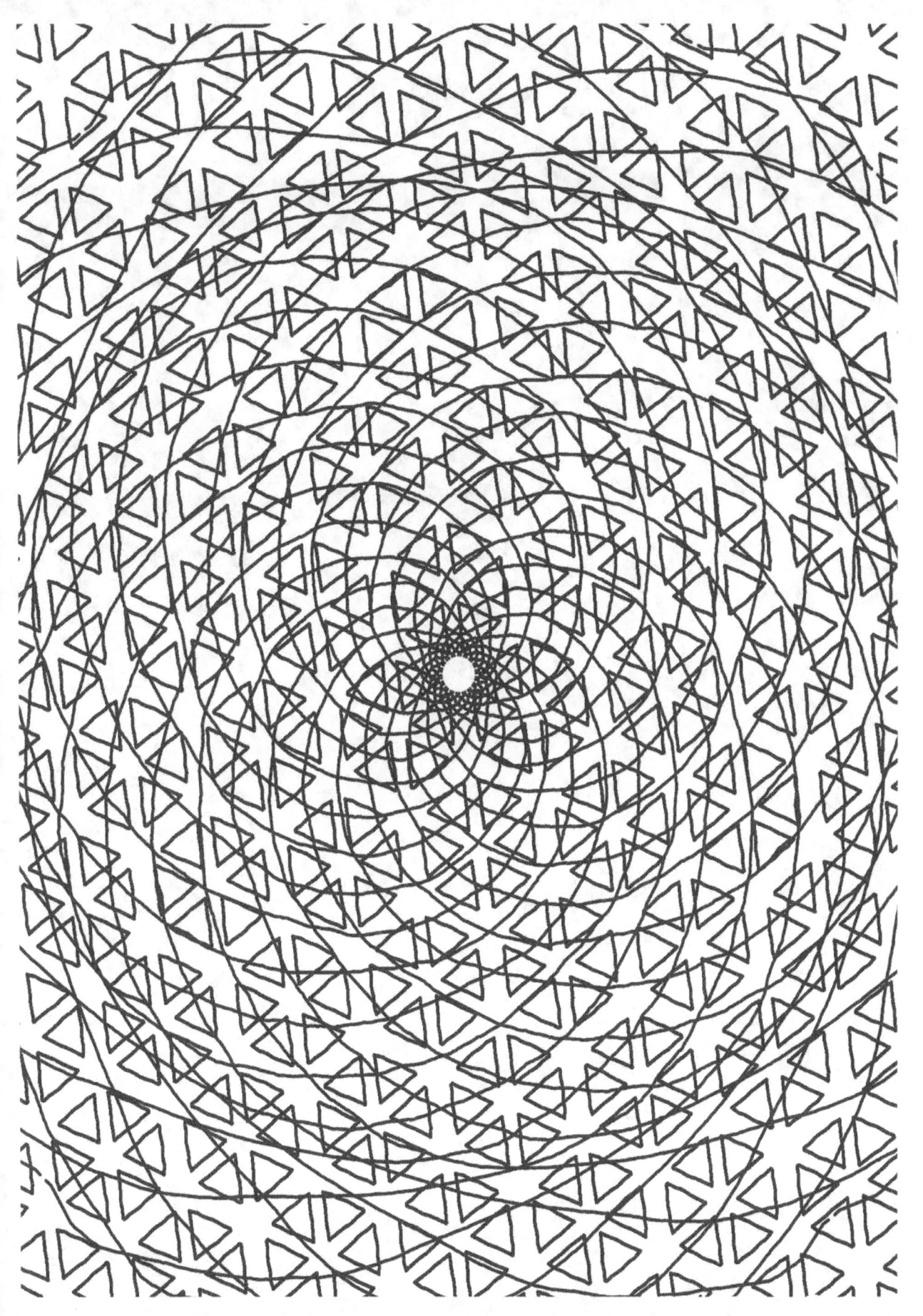

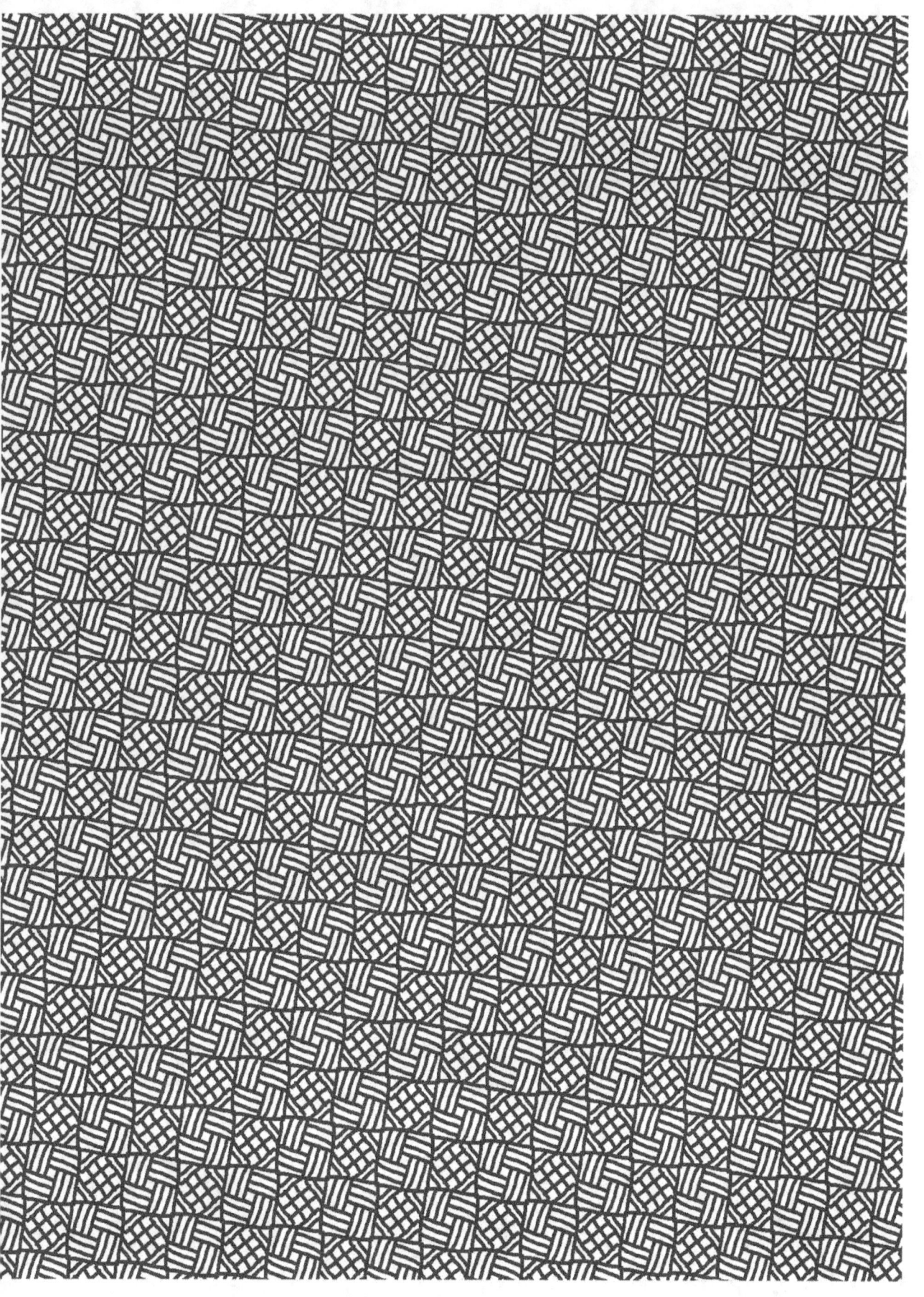

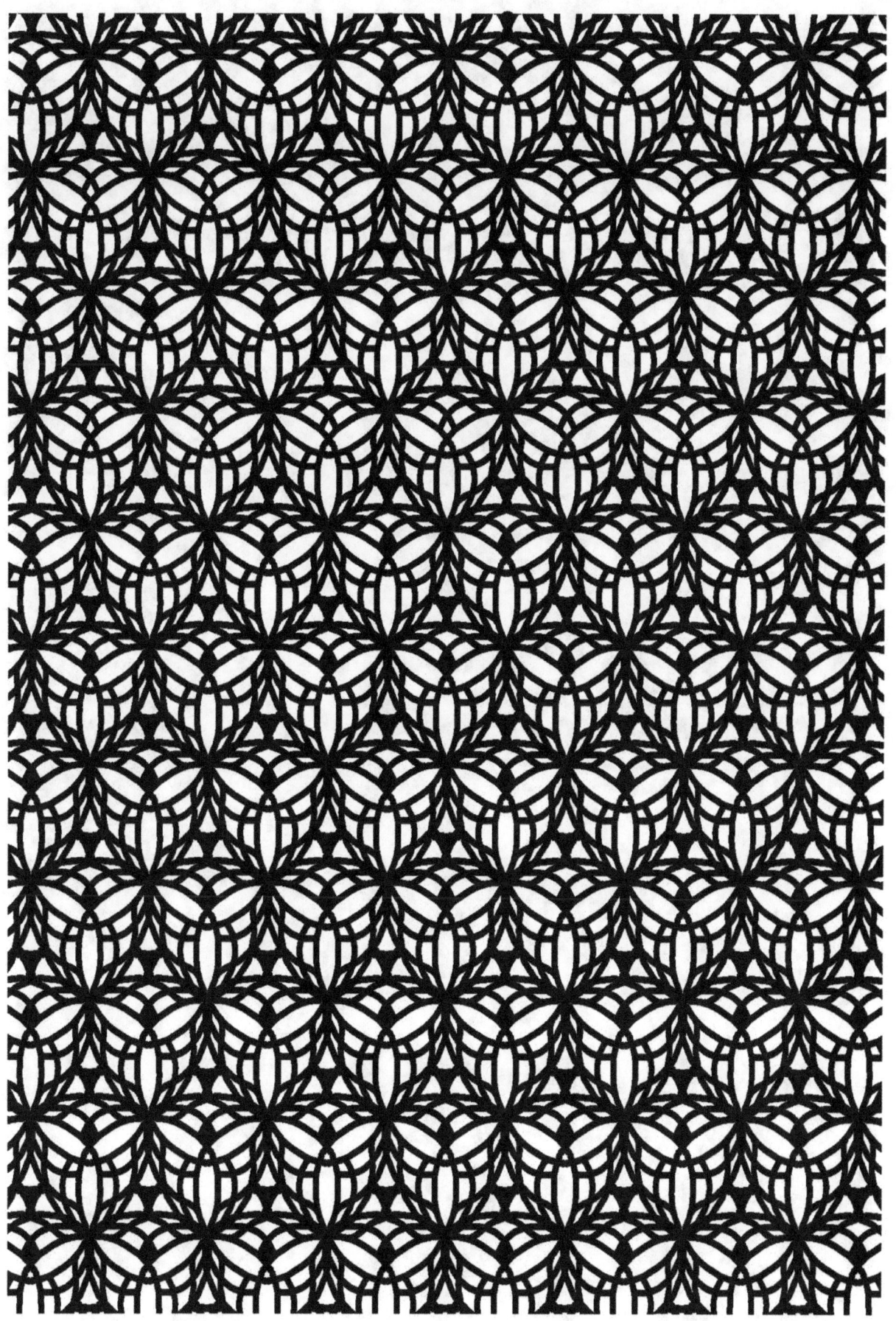

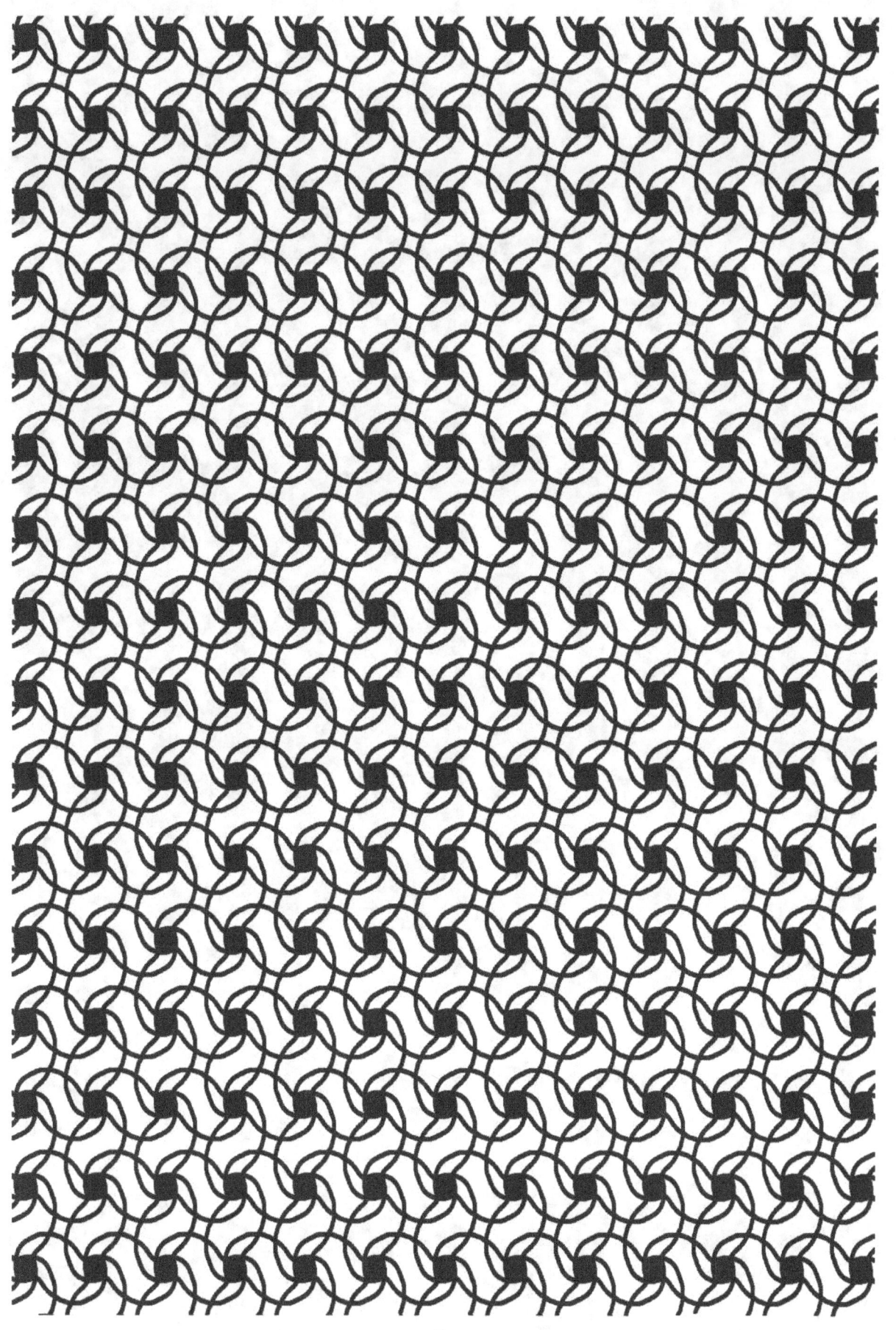

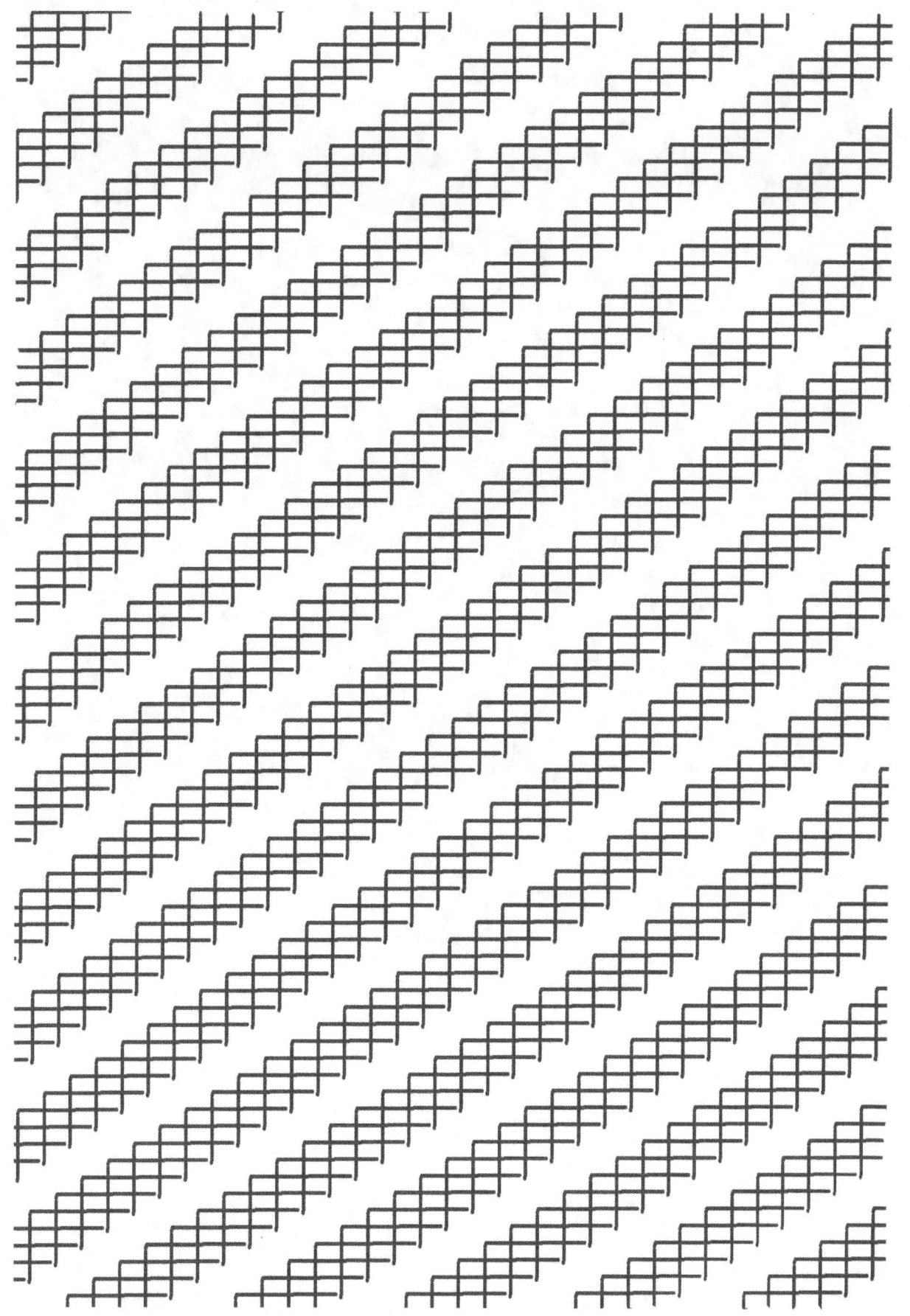

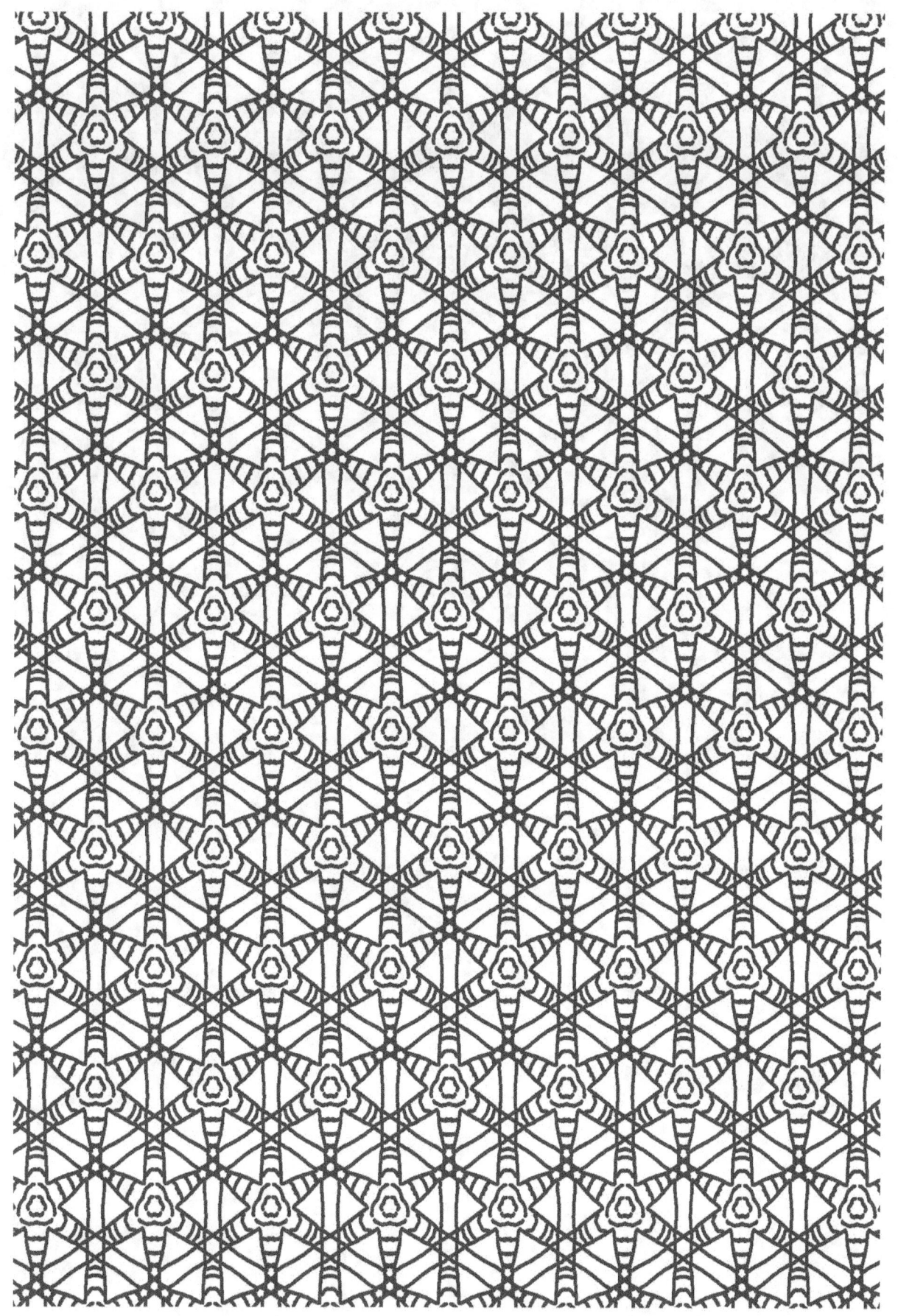

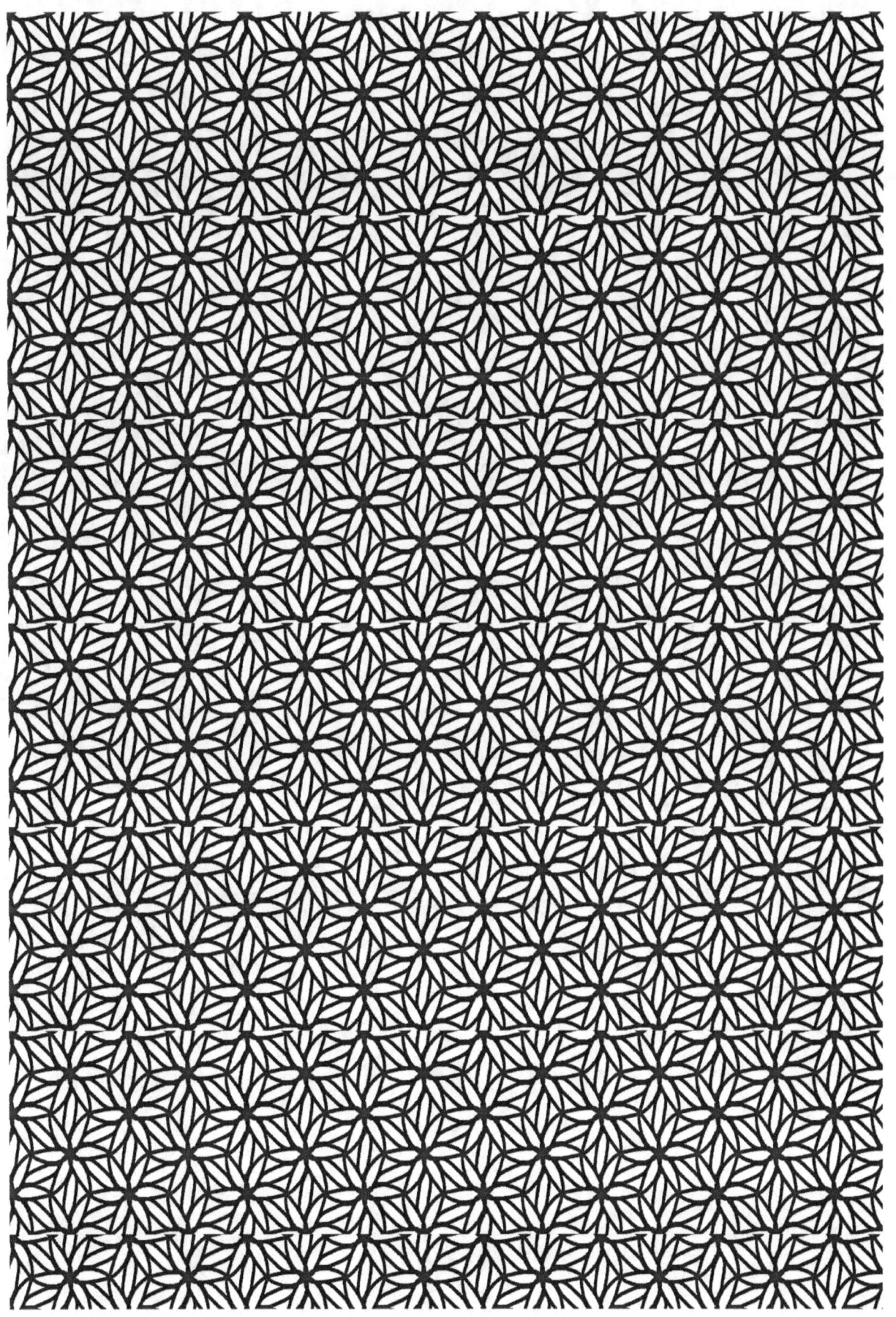

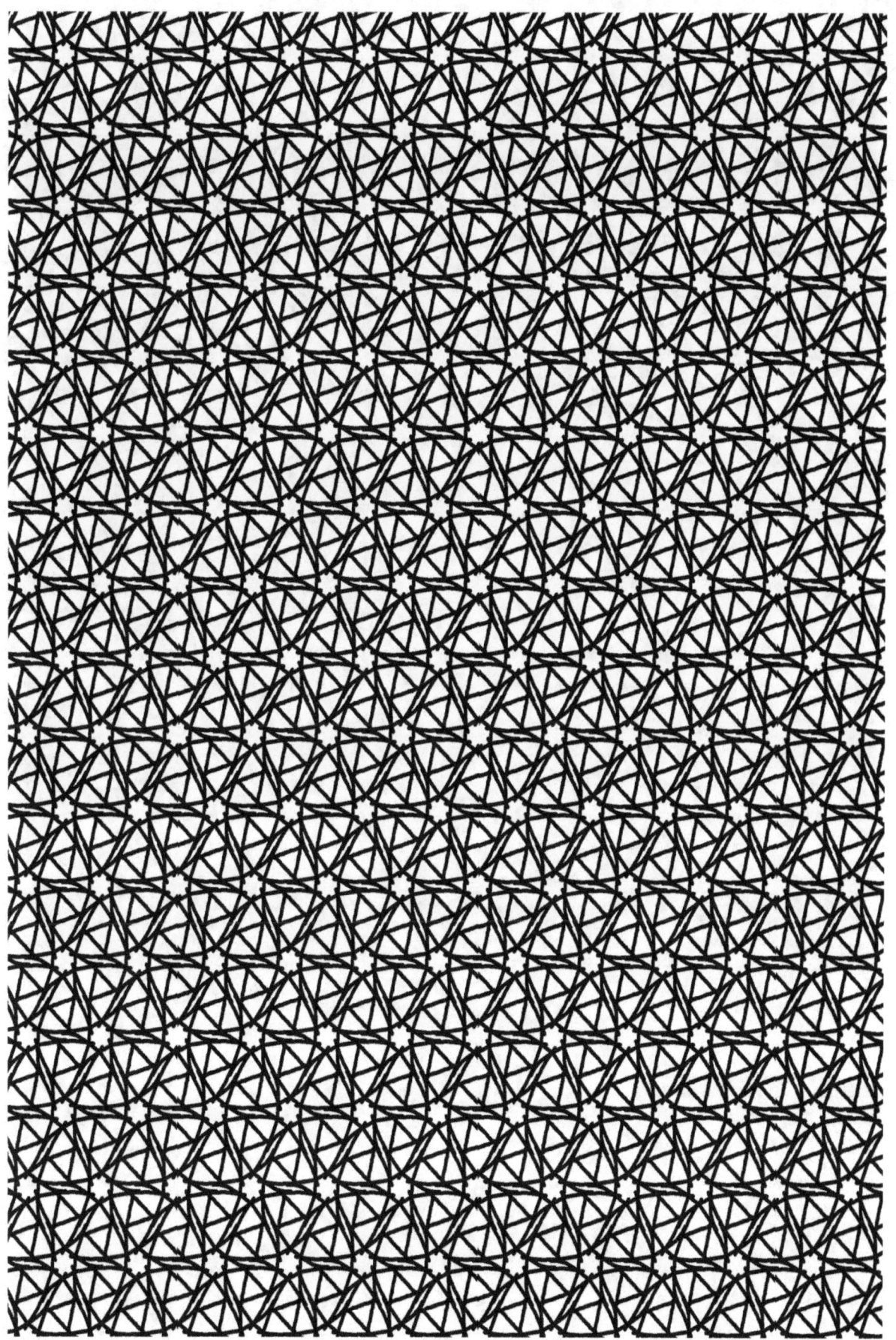

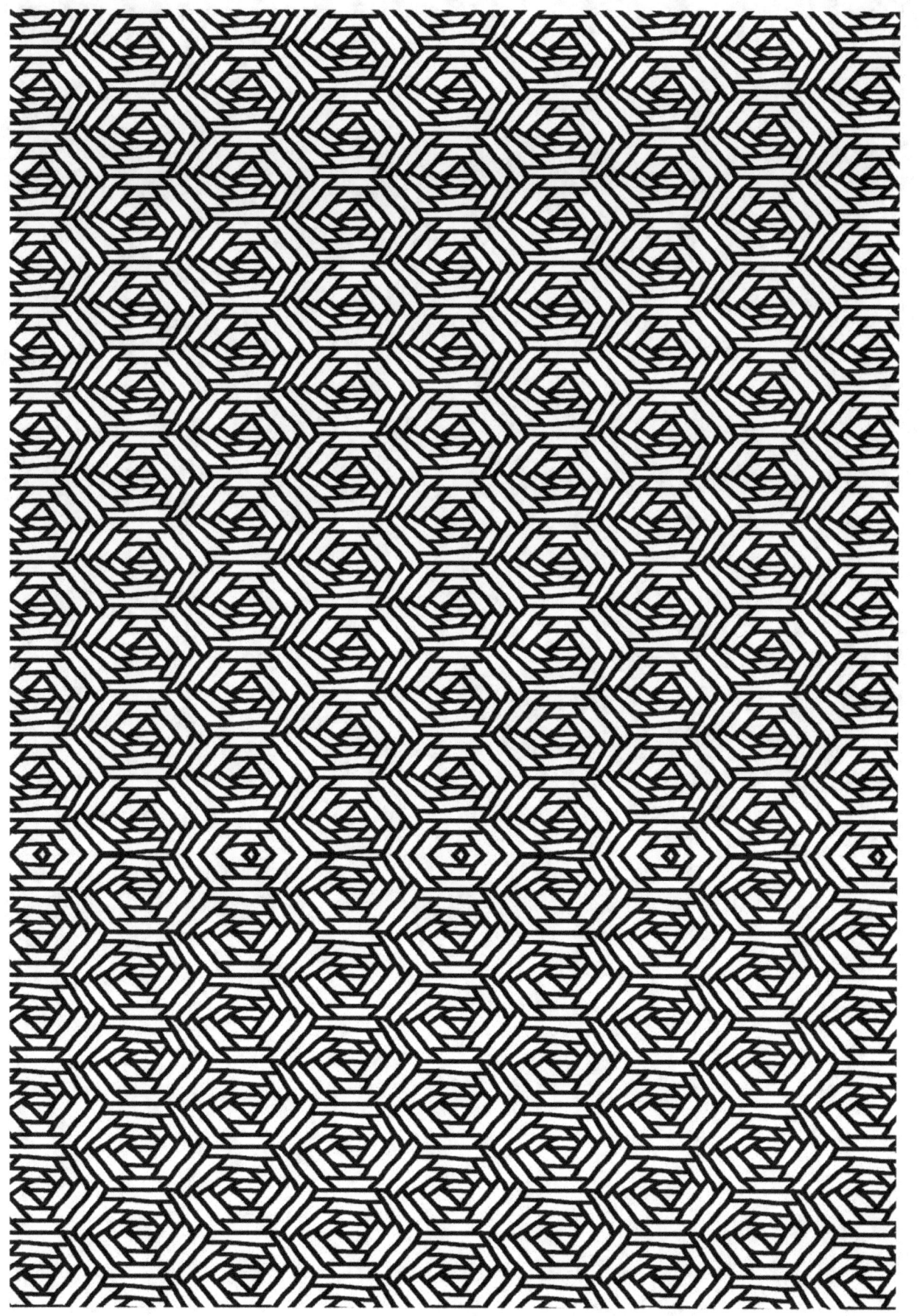

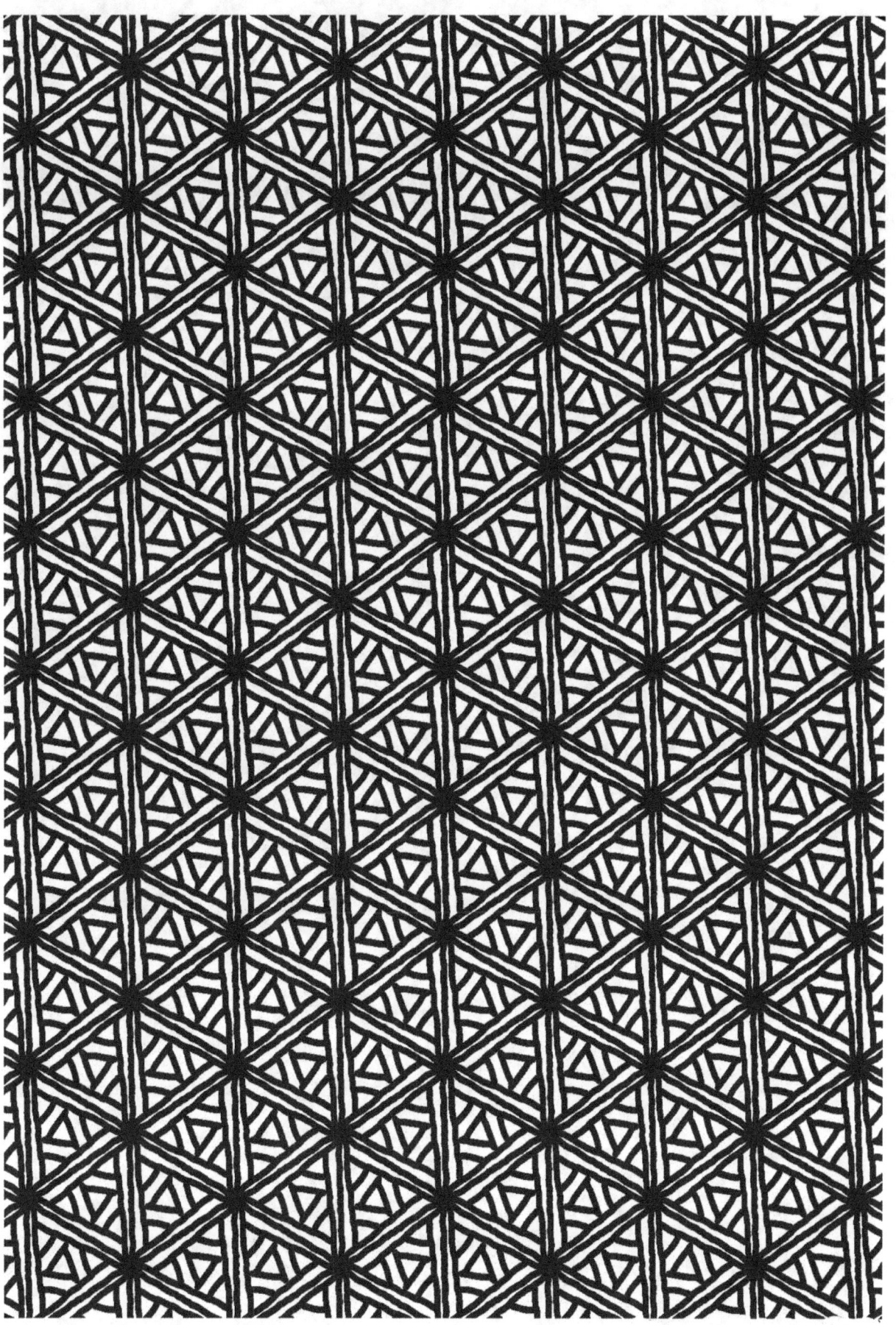

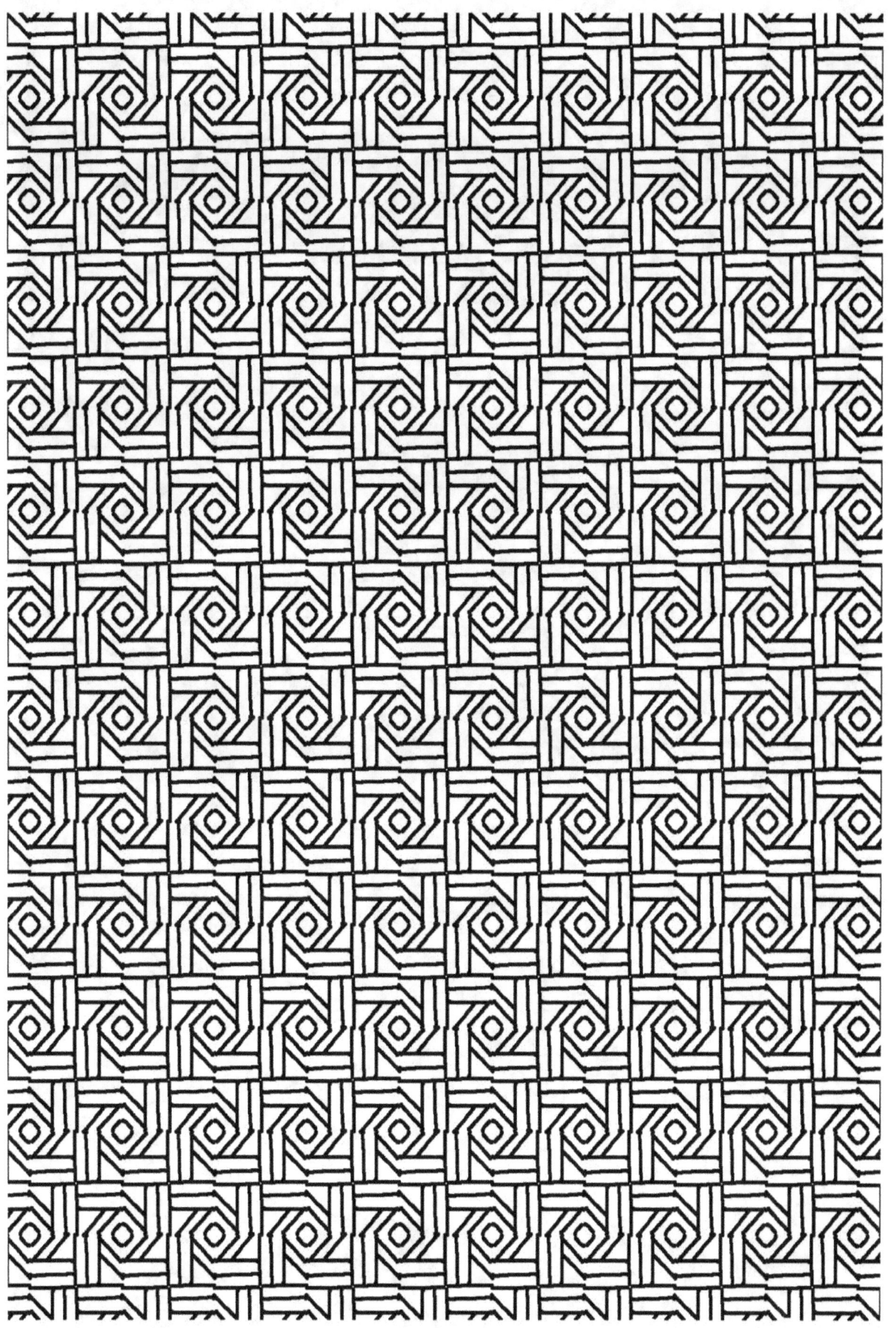

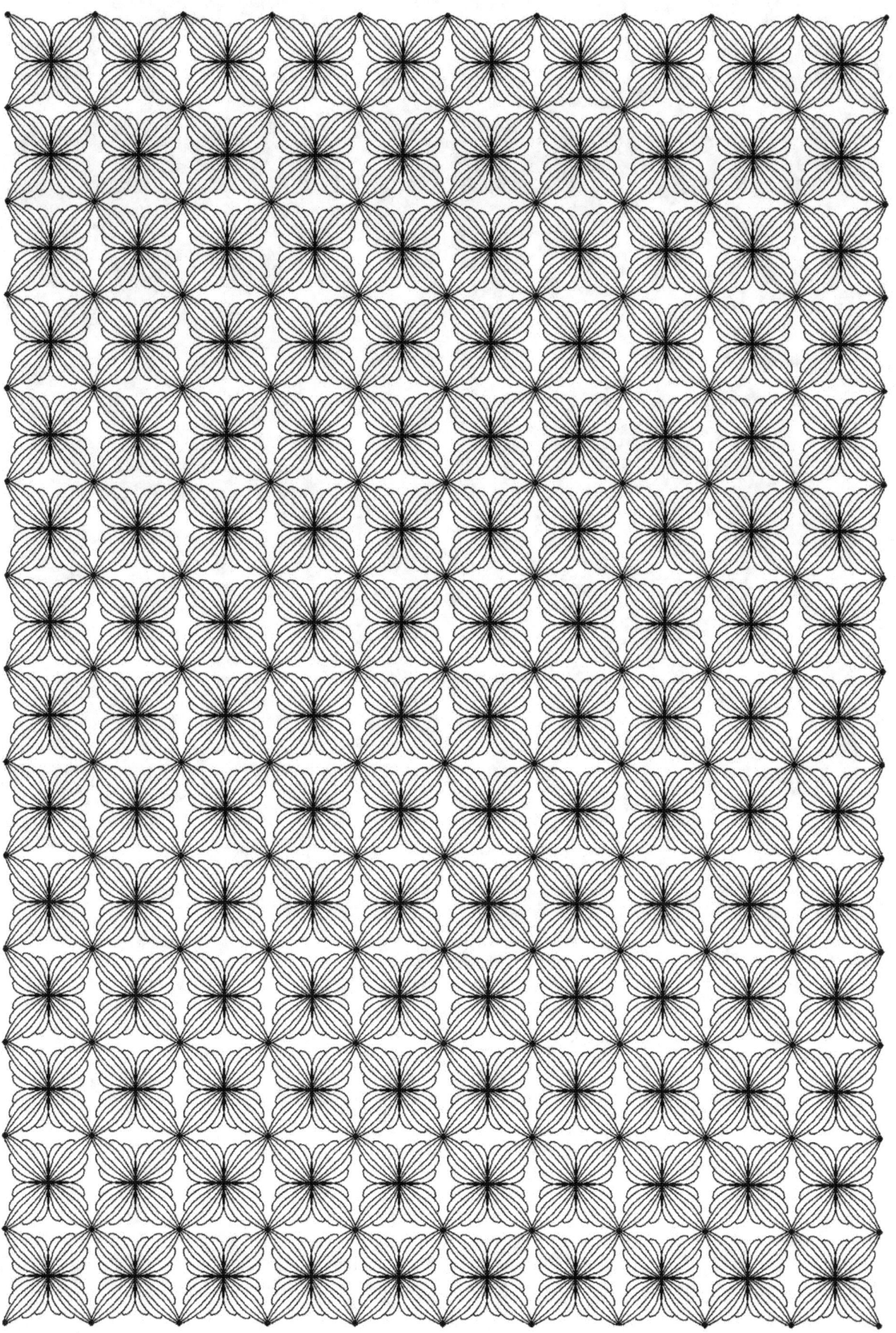

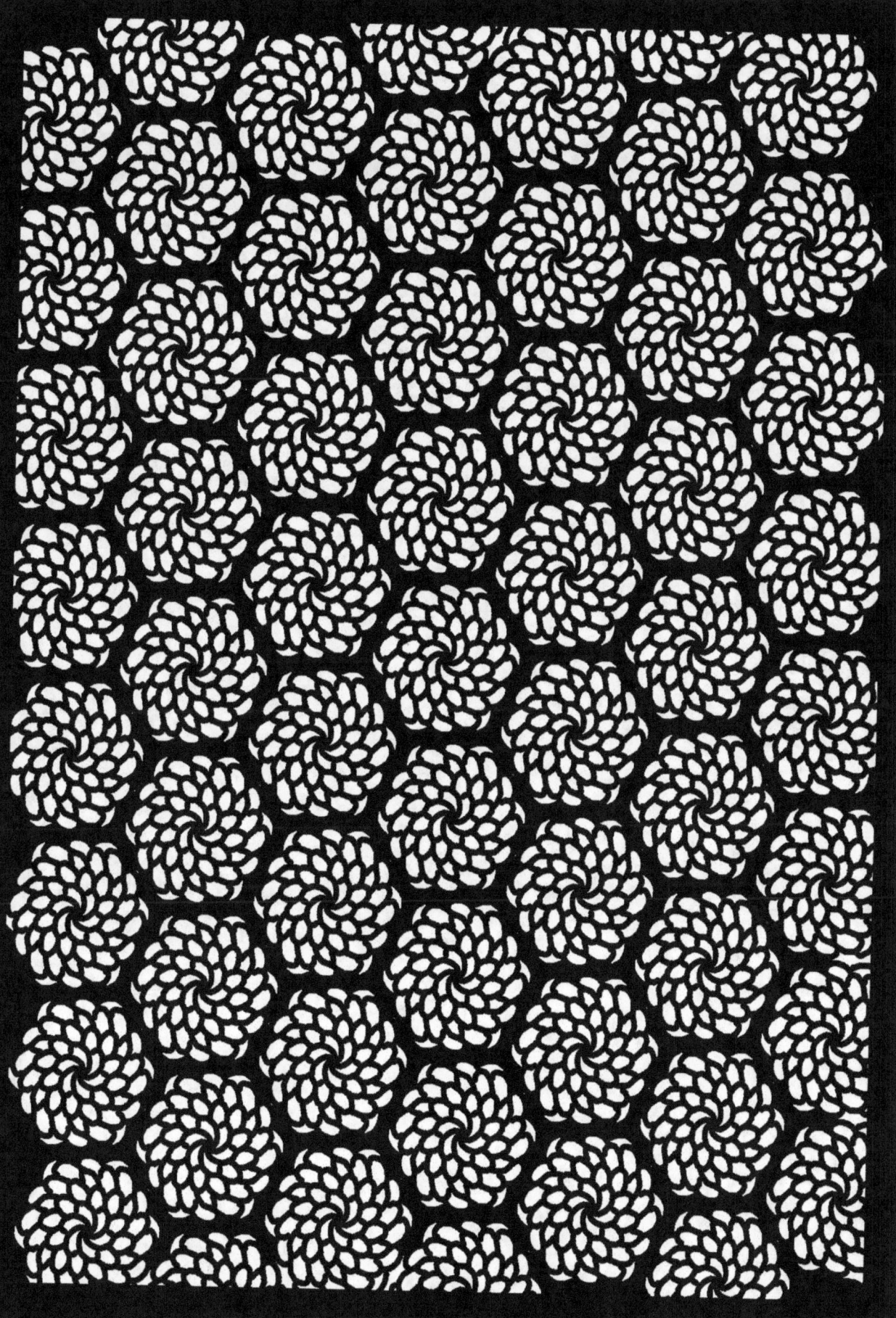

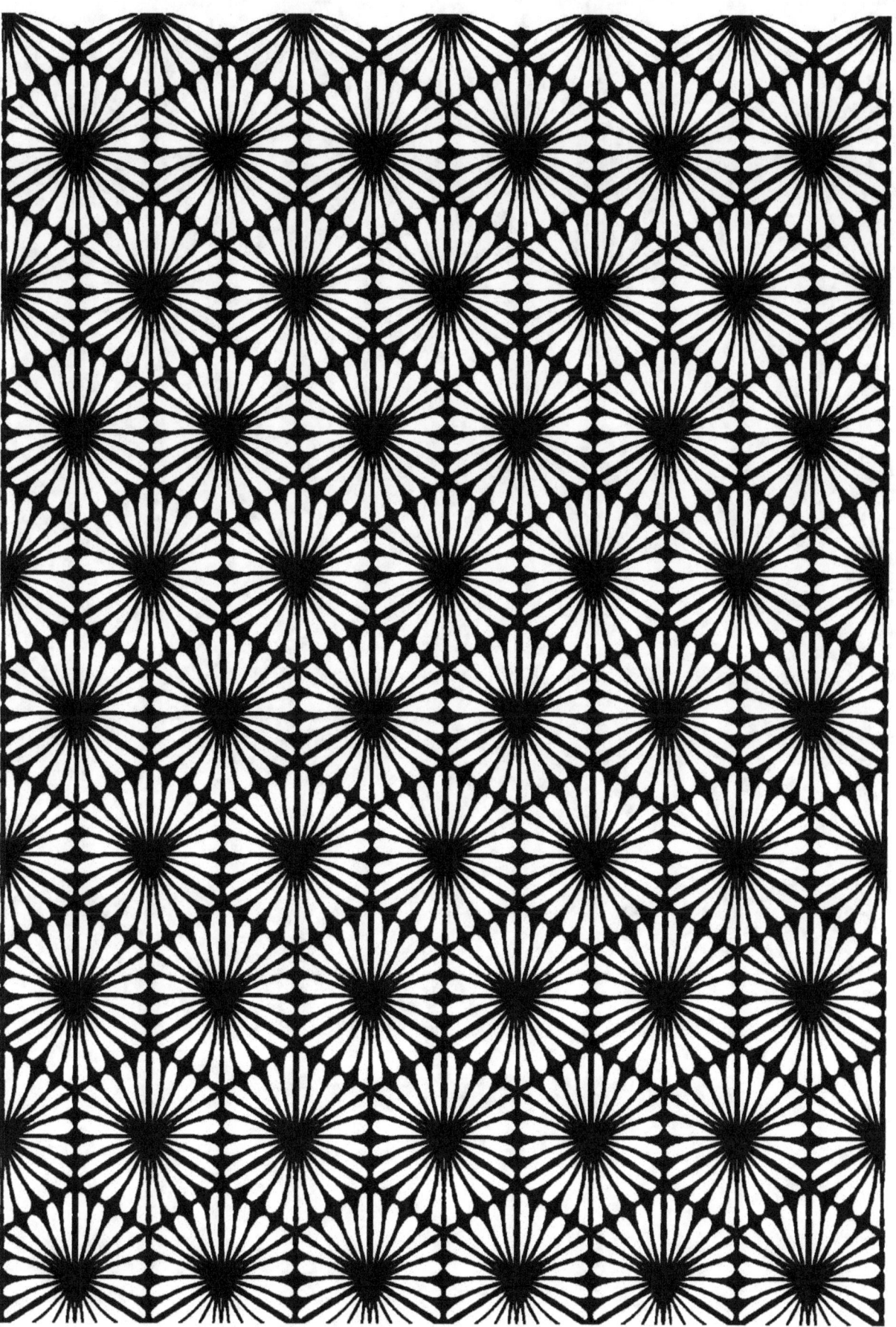

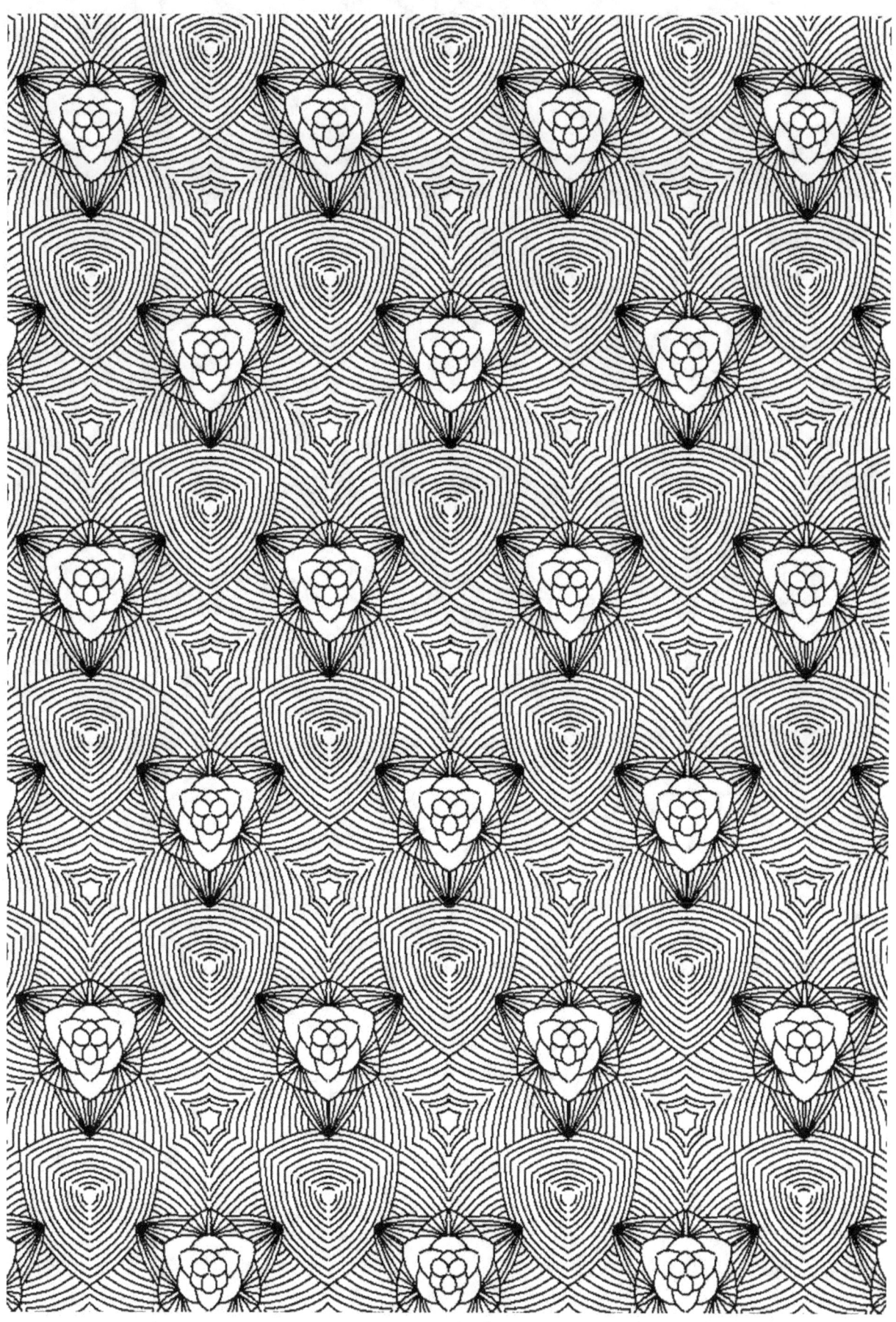

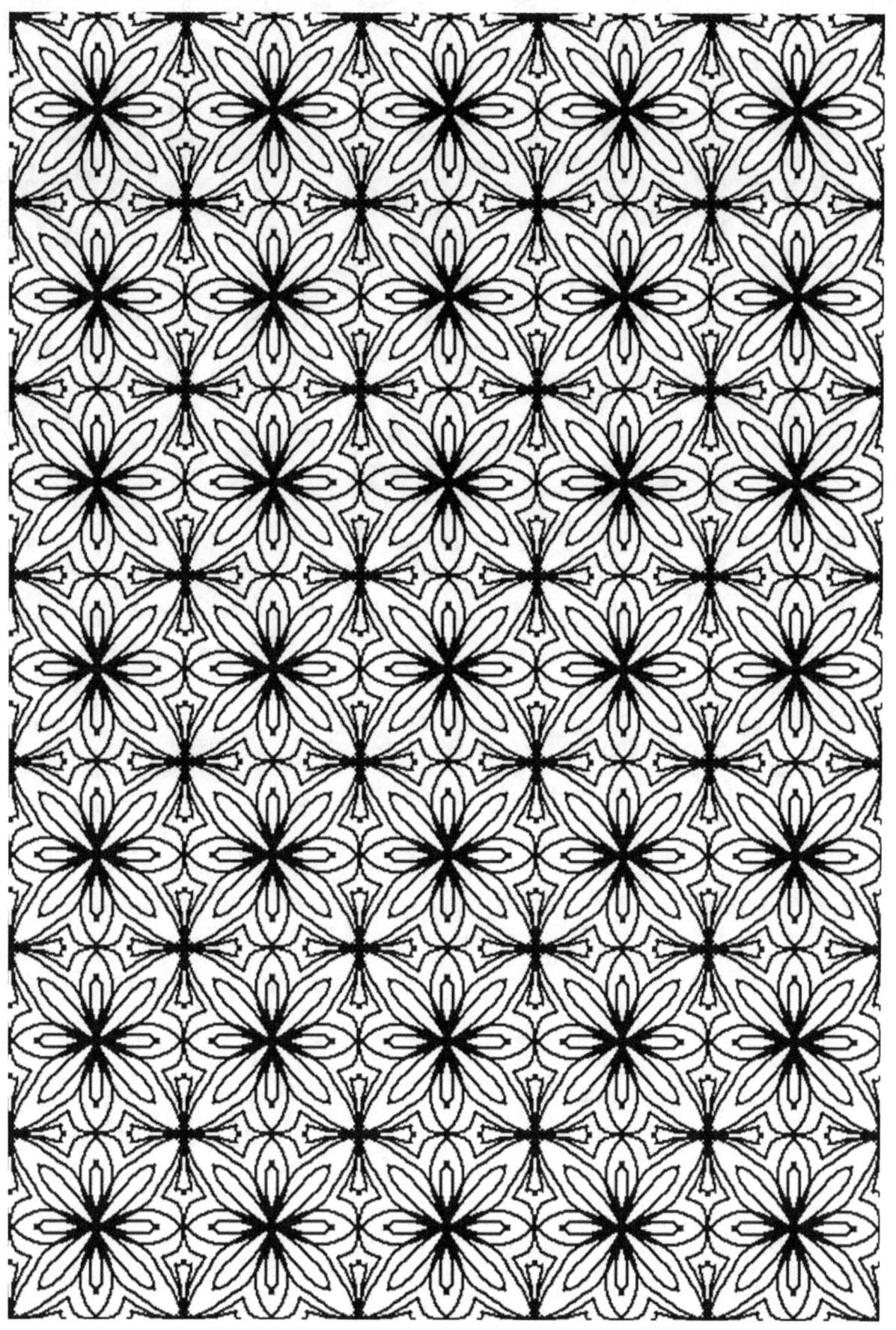

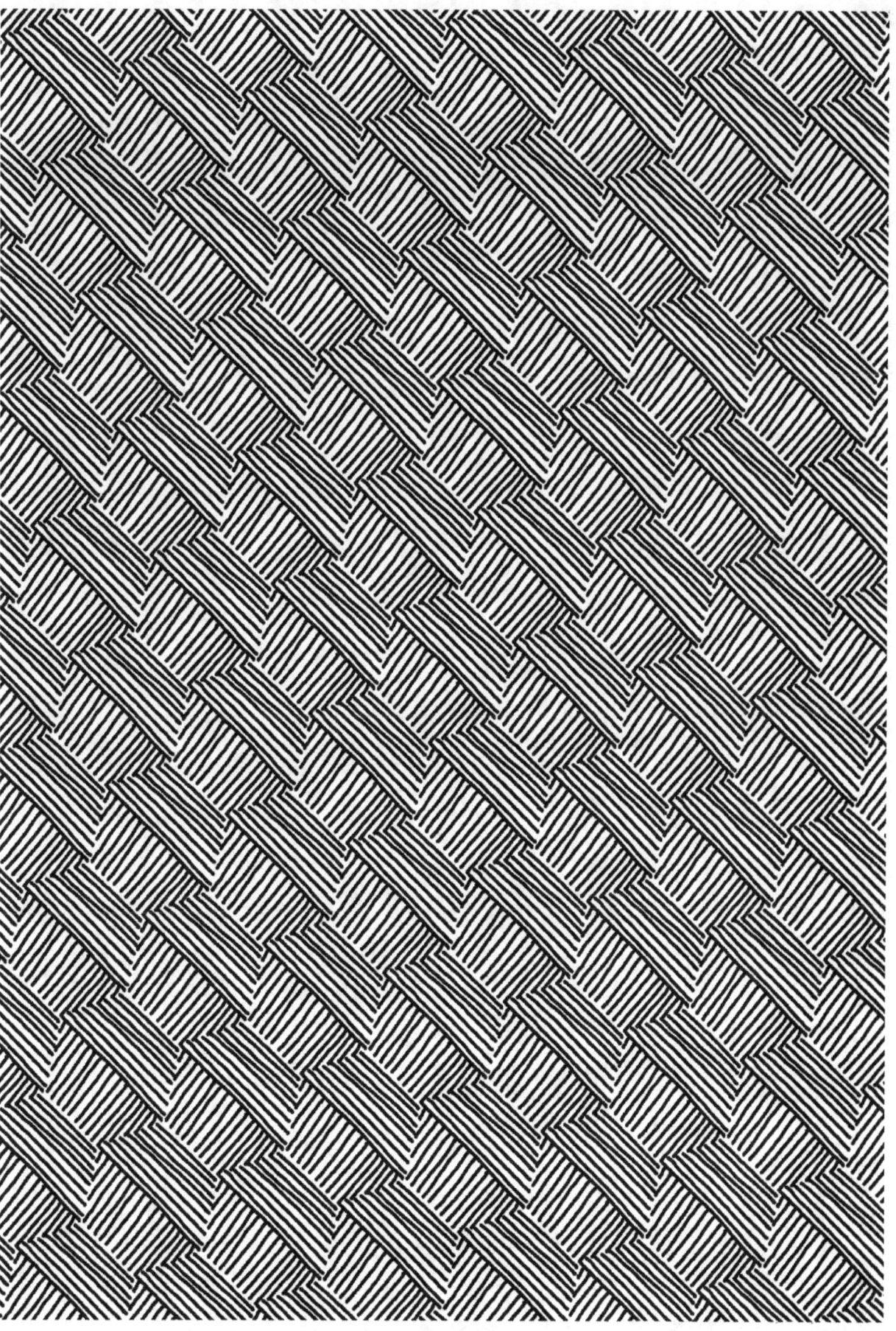

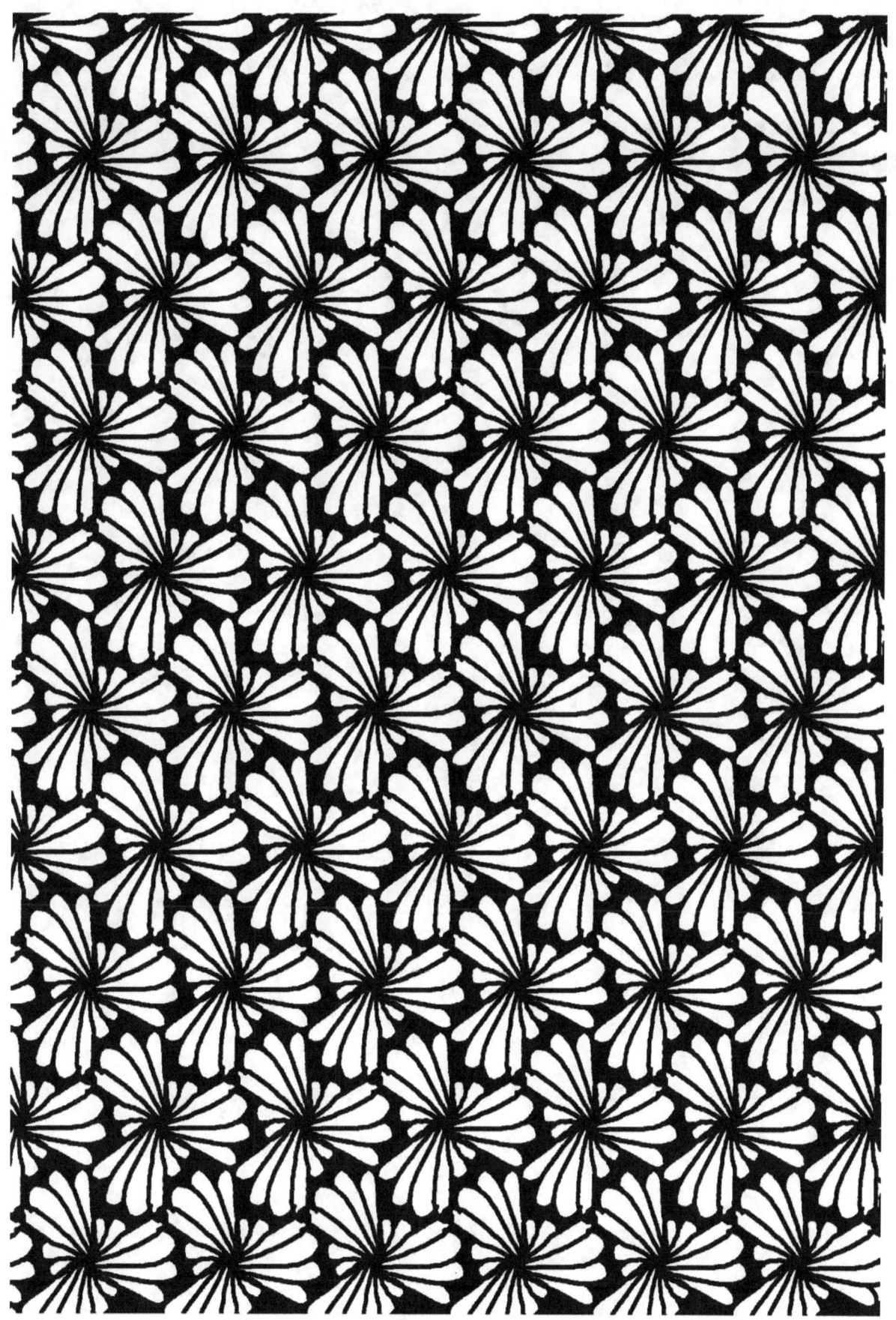

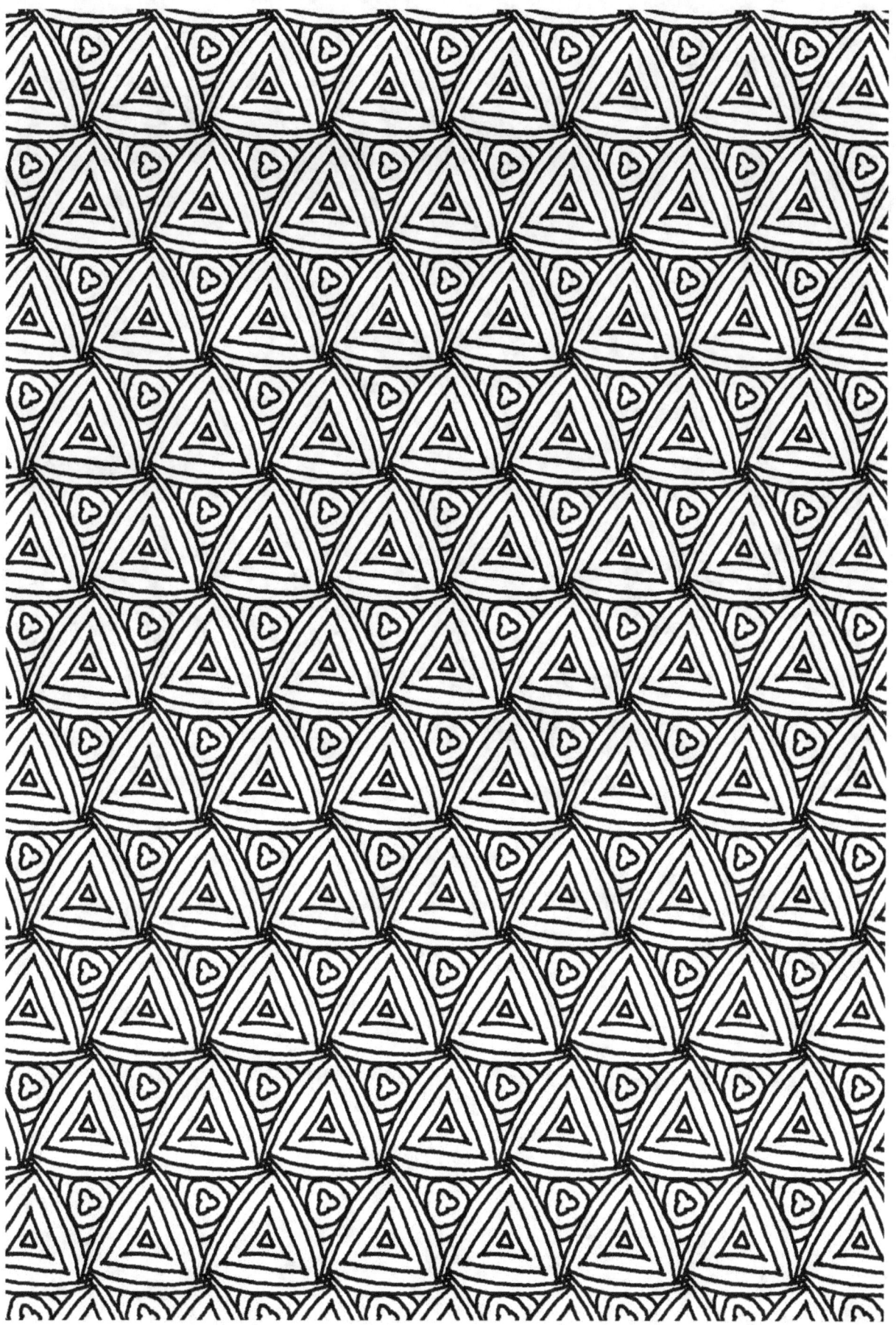

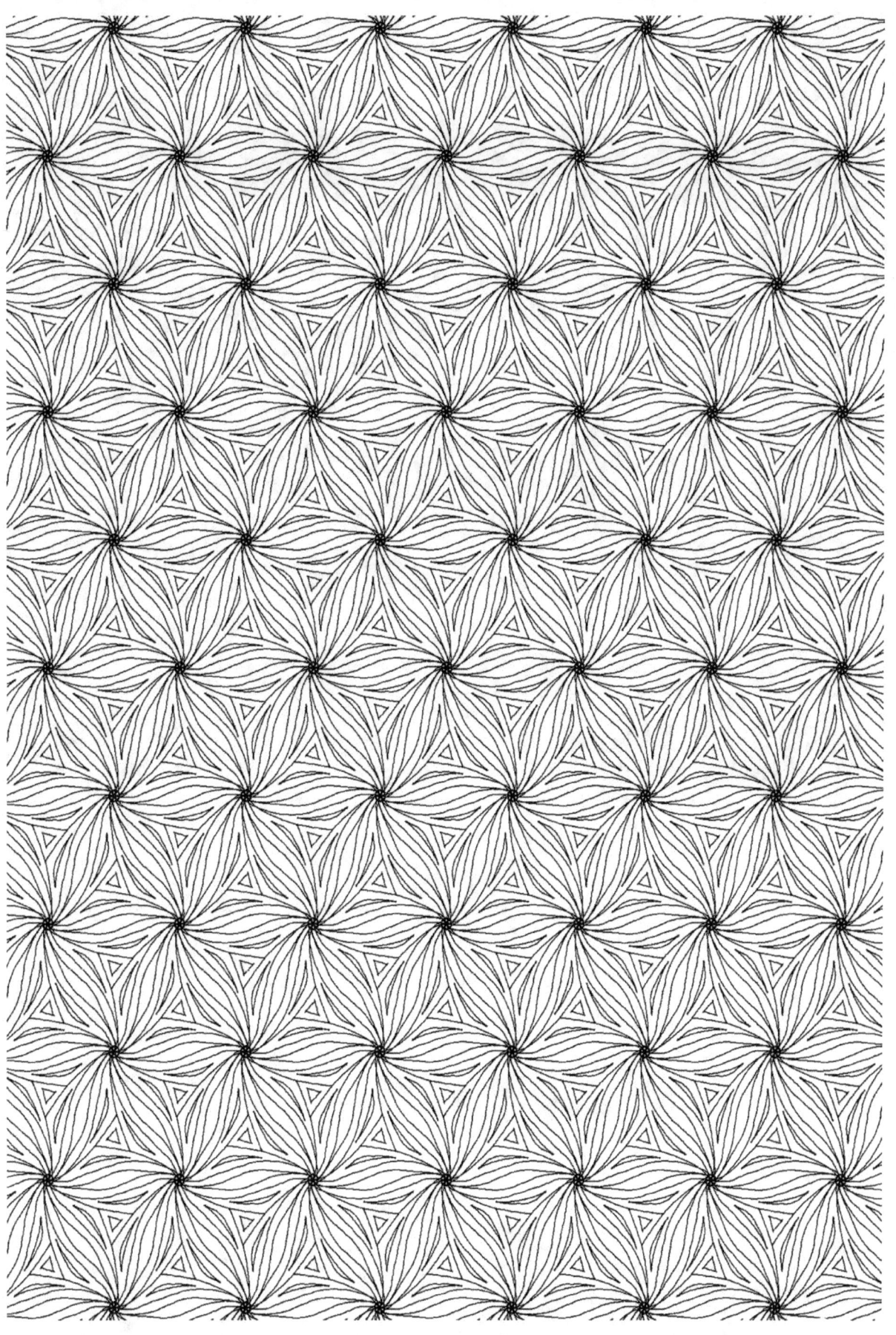

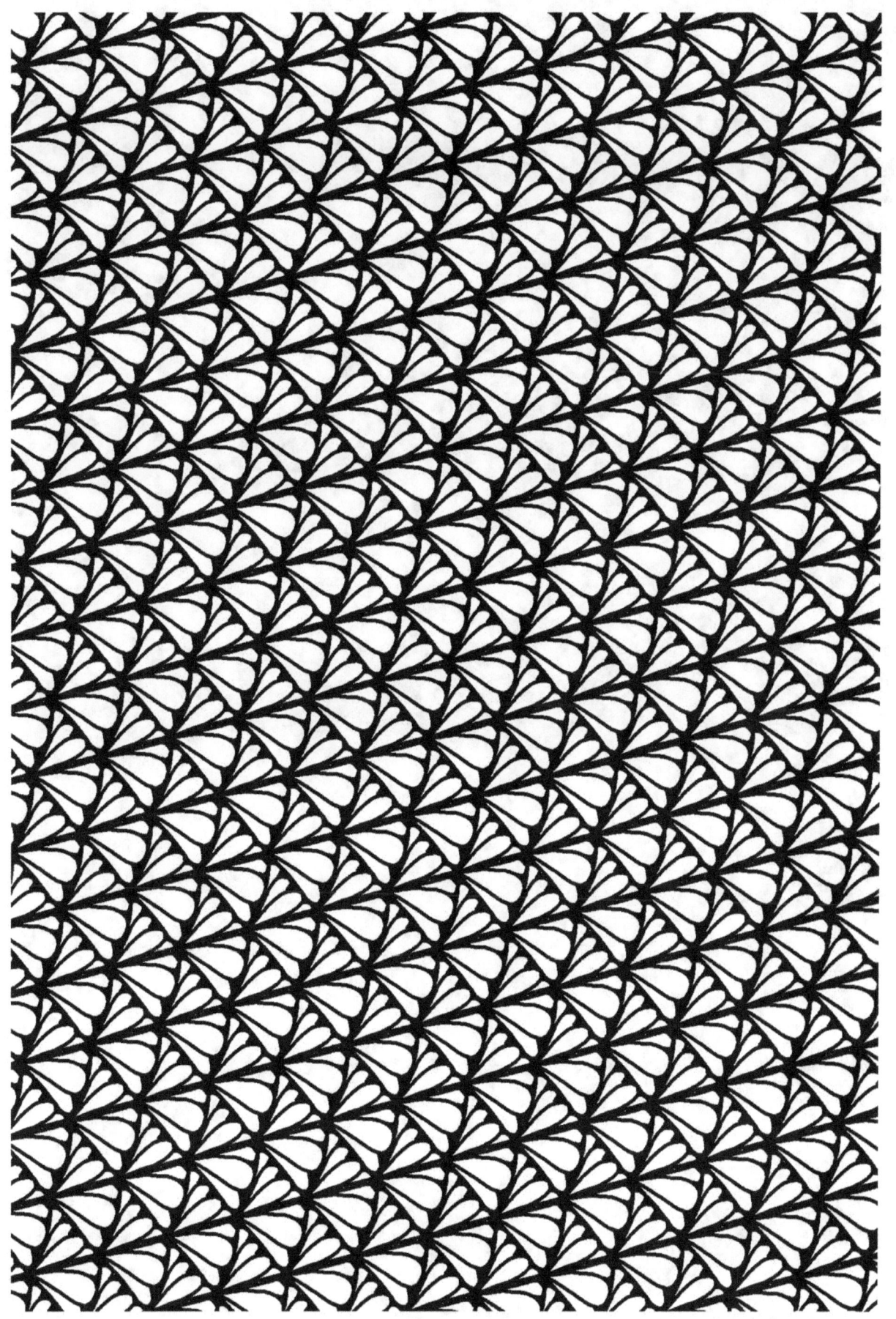

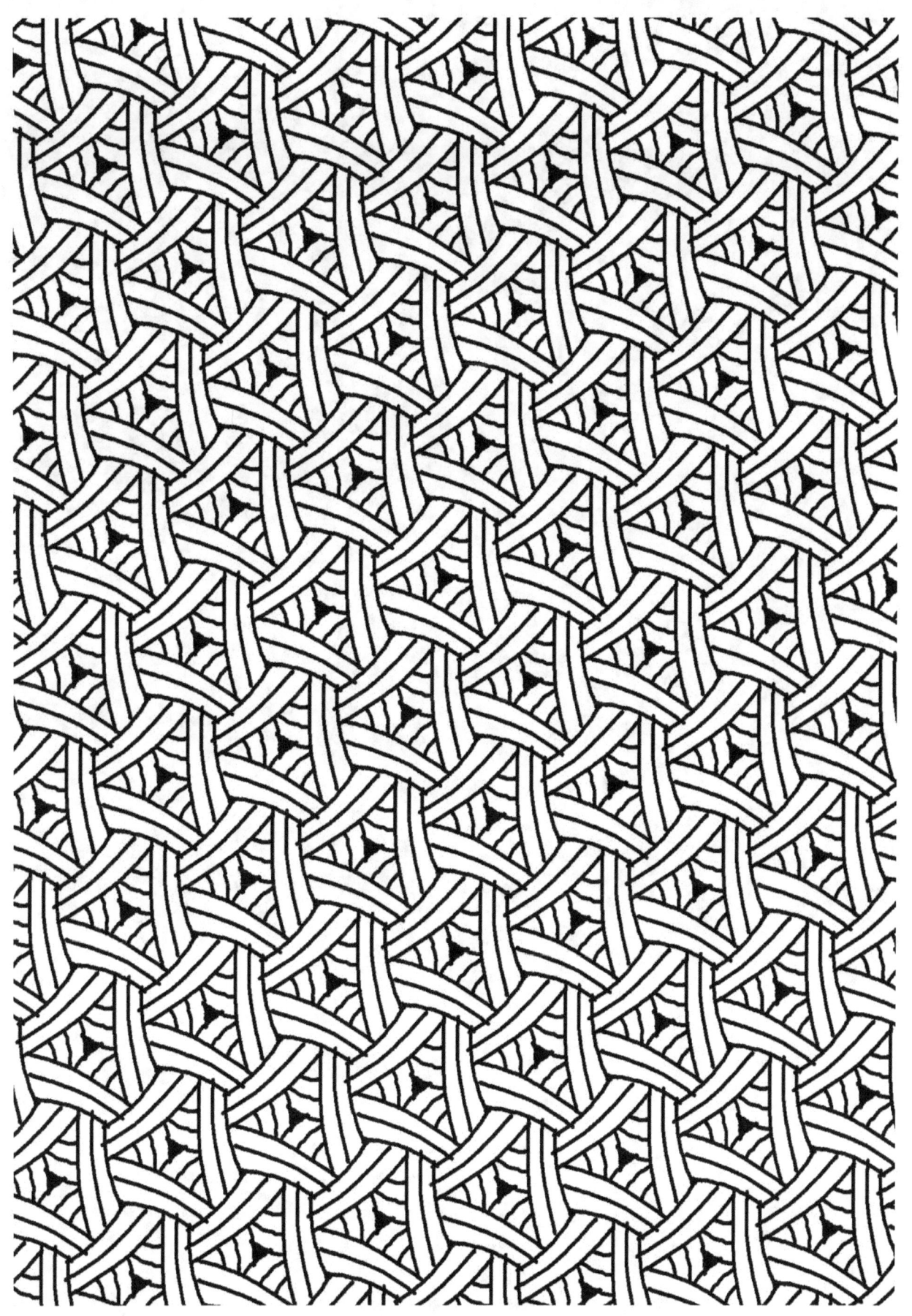

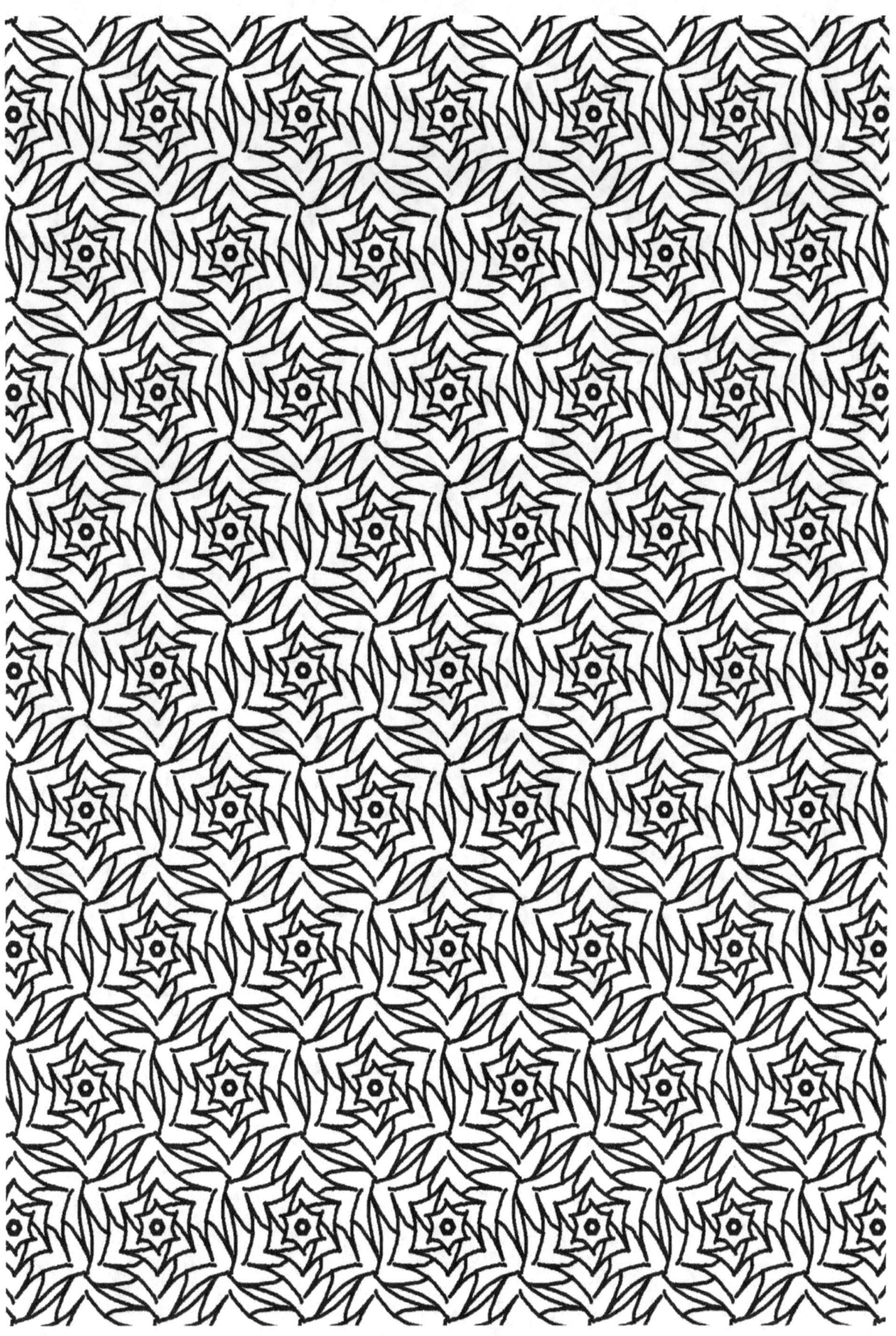

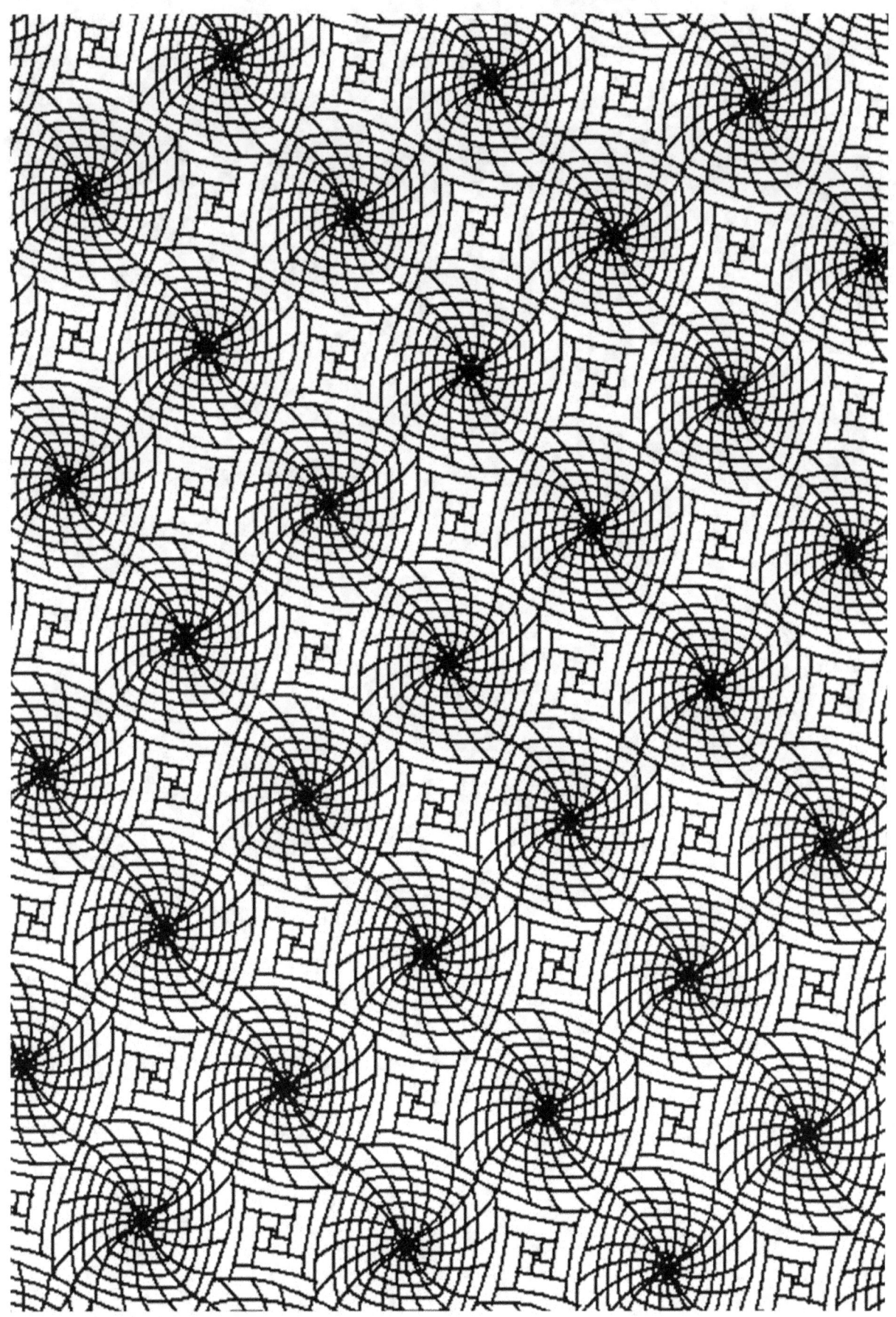

www.ingramcontent.com/pod-product-compliance
Lightning Source LLC
Chambersburg PA
CBHW081736170526
45167CB00009B/3835